LIFE SKILLS FOR KIDS

HOW TO LEARN SOCIAL SKILLS, DEAL WITH
STRONG EMOTIONS, MAKE FRIENDS, EXCEL IN
SCHOOL, MANAGE BULLYING, BUILD
CONFIDENCE, STAY HEALTHY, COOK, CLEAN AND
EVERYTHING IN BETWEEN

GRACE DANIELS

CONTENTS

ALSO BY GRACE DANIELS

Life Skills for Teenage Girls

Life Skills for Teenage Boys

The Growth Mindset for Kids

The Growth Mindset for Teens

Coming Soon:

Building Confident, Brave and Beautiful Girls

Inspring Stories for Confident, Brave and Beautiful Girls

Inspring Stories for Kind, Confident and Brave Boys

Career Planning for Teens

Social Skills for Teens

INTRODUCTION
WHAT ARE LIFE SKILLS?

Anything that teaches you how to deal with things on your own is called a life skill. These are skills that help you learn how to do things like how to deal with bullies, how to make and save money, and cooking. Life skills help you become more independent and responsible.

I wrote this book so you can learn all the skills that will help you throughout the rest of your life. These tips will help you learn to do things on your own, and they are things that even school won't teach you. Learning life skills will also help you handle new situations better. You will be able to solve problems and think of new ways to do things. And as you grow up, these skills will help you be successful and happy.

If you don't learn these skills, it might be harder for you to do things on your own. You might need more help from others, and that can make you feel frustrated.

For example, if you didn't ever learn how to make your own breakfast, you would have to wait for someone else to help you out. Meaning that you waste time and sit around with a grumbling stomach.

In this book, you will learn lots of cool life skills that will help you in your daily life. Including:

- How to deal with big emotions
- What social skills are
- Tips for school (friends, teachers, work, and more)
- How to talk to adults
- Tips for cooking
- Ways to make and save money
- How to deal with bullies
- How to make friends
- How to take care of your body
- And more!

So get ready to have fun and learn some new things that will help you become more responsible! Let's jump right in!

CHAPTER 1
A GUIDE TO BIG FEELINGS

The first life skill we will talk about is how to deal with big emotions. Sometimes feelings can be too heavy to even think about. This chapter will go over what these big emotions are, how you can handle them in healthy ways, and calming activities when things get too crazy.

I bet you've felt lots of different emotions before, like happiness, sadness, anger, fear, or surprise. Did you know that these are called the five primary emotions? (Morin, 2021)

It's important to learn how to handle these big feelings, so let's talk about what each of these emotions mean and how you can deal with them in a healthy way.

Happiness is when you feel really good inside. It can make you feel joyful, content, or proud. For example, when you play with your friends, you might feel happy and joyful. When you're snuggled up with a cozy blanket and a good book, you might feel happy and content. And when you finally score a soccer goal or win the game, you might feel happy and proud. You might smile a lot and feel like you want to dance or jump up and down!

Sadness is when you feel really down and don't want to do anything. It's like when you miss someone you love or when something you want doesn't happen. For example, if your pet gets hurt or lost, you might feel sad and disappointed. If you move to a new town and don't know anyone yet, you might feel sad and lonely. When you are sad you may cry and want to be alone for a little bit.

Anger is when you feel really mad. It's like when someone takes something of yours or when someone is mean to you. For example, if someone takes something that belongs to you without asking, you might feel angry and frustrated. If your little brother keeps bothering you when you're trying to play, you might feel angry and annoyed. And if you feel like you're being treated unfairly, you might feel angry and resentful. You might find yourself wanting to yell at someone or hit something, but it's much more healthy to try and take a deep breath and calm down instead.

Fear is when you feel really scared. It's like when you hear a loud noise or when you see something that looks scary. Fear can make you feel things like nervousness, anxiety, or terror. For example, if you're about to start at a new school and don't know anyone yet, you might feel fearful and nervous. If there's a loud thunderstorm outside and you're scared of thunder, you might feel fearful and anxious. And if a big, scary dog is chasing you, you might feel fearful. You might feel like your heart is racing, and your body might feel shaky or sweaty.

Surprise is when something happens that you didn't expect. Surprise can make you feel other things like excitement, confusion, or curiosity. It's like when someone jumps out and says "boo!" or when you get a surprise present!

The thing is that there are more than five emotions. These are just the big ones that can describe almost any feeling you might experience. It's okay to feel all of these emotions in lots of different ways, and it's important to talk to someone you trust if you're feeling overwhelmed or need help processing your feelings.

EXAMPLES OF NOT CONTROLLING YOUR EMOTIONS

Some emotions just feel too big to deal with. One of the biggest steps in growing up is learning how to control your emotions and reactions. Let's start off with some examples of unhealthy emotional reactions:

- If you feel really worried or anxious and start avoiding things that scare you, like going to school or trying new things.
- If you get really angry and start yelling at your friends or family members, that's not handling your feelings in a good or healthy way.
- If you feel really sad and want to stay in your room thinking about how sad you are all day, that is not a healthy way of managing your reactions.
- If you get really scared and start hiding or running away from things that aren't actually dangerous, that's not managing your emotions in a healthy way.
- If you feel embarrassed or ashamed and start hiding or lying about what happened instead of talking to someone about it.
- If you get really excited and start jumping or screaming in a place where it's not appropriate to do this, that is not a good way of controlling your emotions.
- If you feel disappointed or sad and start saying mean things to yourself, like, "I'm stupid," or "I can't do anything right," that's not a good way to handle the situation.
- If you feel really frustrated and start giving up or throwing things instead of trying to find a solution, that's not managing your emotions in a healthy way.

EXAMPLES OF HOW TO CONTROL YOUR EMOTIONS IN A HEALTHY WAY

It's essential to not only try to understand and express your emotions, but also to learn healthy ways to cope with them. Managing your emotions in a healthy way means finding ways to express how you feel without hurting yourself or others. Always remember that it is okay to ask for help or take a break when you need it (Morin, 2021).

- If you feel angry, you can take a deep breath and count to ten before talking about how you feel.
- If you feel sad, you can talk to someone you trust, like a parent or a teacher, about what's bothering you.
- If you feel scared, you can remind yourself that you're safe and try to think of things that make you feel happy or calm.
- If you feel excited, you can share your excitement with others, but also remember to take turns and listen to what they have to say.
- If you feel worried or anxious, you can try to imagine the best-case scenario instead of the worst-case scenario, and think of things that make you feel brave and strong.
- If you feel frustrated, you can take a break from what you're doing and try again later, or ask for help from someone you trust.
- If you feel happy, you can share your happiness with others, but also remember to be considerate of their feelings and take turns.
- If you feel embarrassed or ashamed, you can talk to someone you trust about what happened and try to learn from your mistakes.
- If you feel overwhelmed, you can take a deep breath and remind yourself that it's okay to take things one step at a time.
- If you feel proud of something you've done, you can celebrate your accomplishment but also remember to be humble and appreciate the help and support of others.

If you are having a hard time changing your behaviors, the next section talks about REAL steps you can take and activities you can practice to calm yourself down and manage your emotions in a healthy way!

CALMING ACTIVITIES

If you are feeling overwhelmed, angry, or unable to calm yourself, you might not know what to do with your feelings. Below are a few calming activities you can come back to when you can't handle what you are feeling.

Take deep breaths — When you're feeling upset or anxious, taking deep breaths can help you calm down. Take a deep breath in through your nose, hold it for a few seconds, and then slowly exhale through your mouth.

Listen to calming music— Listening to soothing music can help you relax and feel more centered. Choose music that makes you feel happy and calm, and listen to it in a quiet place.

Draw or color— Drawing and coloring can be very therapeutic and calming. You can draw or color anything you like, and it doesn't matter if it's not perfect.

Practice yoga or stretching— Yoga and stretching can help you release tension and feel more relaxed. You can try simple yoga poses or stretches like touching your toes or reaching up to the sky.

Go for a walk in nature— Being in nature can be very calming and grounding. Take a walk in a park, forest, or another natural setting, and pay attention to the sights, sounds, and smells around you.

Write in a journal— Writing down your thoughts and feelings can help you process them and feel more centered. You can write about anything that's on your mind or use prompts to help you get started.

Take a warm bath or shower— Taking a warm bath or shower can be very relaxing and soothing. Use your favorite bubble bath or bath salts, and take your time to enjoy the warmth and quiet.

Practice mindfulness— Mindfulness means being present in the moment and paying attention to your thoughts, feelings, and surroundings. You can practice mindfulness by focusing on your breath, noticing the sensations in your body, or paying attention to your surroundings.

Play with a pet— Playing with a pet can be very calming and comforting. If you have a dog, cat, or other pet, spend some time petting them, playing with them, or just sitting with them.

Do something creative— Doing something creative like writing a story, making a craft, or playing music can be very calming and rewarding. Choose an activity that you enjoy and that makes you feel happy and relaxed.

At the end of some of the chapters you will have journaling questions and ideas so you can think deeper about what we talk about! You might want to have a separate diary, notebook, or journal for the questions in this book just to keep everything organized. Let's get into the questions for this section that will help you process these big emotions:

QUESTIONS FOR YOUR JOURNAL— THINKING ABOUT THESE BIG EMOTIONS

1. Write about a time when you felt really angry. What made you feel angry? How did you handle your anger? Was there something you could have done differently to manage your anger in a healthy way?
2. Think about a time when you felt really sad. What made you feel sad? How did you cope with your sadness? Did talking to someone or doing something you enjoy help you feel better?
3. Write about a time when you felt really scared. What made you feel scared? How did you deal with your fear? Did you talk to someone about your fears or try to do something that made you feel safer?
4. Think about a time when you felt really happy. What made you feel happy? How did you express your happiness? Did you do something to celebrate or share your happiness with others?
5. Write about a time when you felt really stressed or overwhelmed. What made you feel stressed or overwhelmed? How did you manage your stress? Did you take a break, talk to someone, or do something calming to help you feel better?

Remember that it's okay to feel all kinds of feelings. Everyone gets angry, sad, or scared sometimes, and that's normal. The important thing is to know how to manage your emotions in a healthy way.

Managing your emotions in a healthy way will be a big part of growing up! The tips above are always here to help you figure it out along the way. Next, we will talk about what social skills are, how they can help you be more confident, and how they can help you make friends!

CHAPTER 2
SOCIAL SKILLS

Social skills are things that help you interact with other people. They include things like making friends, sharing your things, taking turns, and listening to others. It's awesome to learn social skills because they help you communicate and get along with others. When you have good social skills, you can make friends easily, work well in groups, and people like you better.

For example, if you have good sharing skills, you can easily take turns with a new video game with your friends without fighting over it. If you have good listening skills, you can understand what others are saying and answer in a way that makes sense, which helps you get along better with others.

Learning social skills also helps you feel more confident and comfortable in social situations. When you know how to be around others in a positive way, you feel more in control and less nervous or scared.

This chapter is about different social skills you can start learning today, how to practice them, and what they do to help your life. Let's dive right in!

ACTIVE LISTENING AND CONVERSATION SKILLS

Have you ever been talking to someone, and they're not really listening to you? Maybe they're looking around or playing with their phone instead of paying attention to what you're saying. That doesn't feel very good, does it?

That's why it's important to learn about active listening and conversational skills. When you use these skills, you can have better conversations and build stronger relationships with others. Active listening means that you're really paying attention to the person who is talking (and showing them that you are listening to them). This means:

- Making eye contact
- Facing the person who is speaking
- And using body language that shows you're interested. You can also nod your head or say "uh-huh" to show that you're listening (Homer, 2021).

9

QUICK TIP: WHAT IS BODY LANGUAGE?

Body language is the way you use your body to tell others how you are feeling. For example, if you're happy, you might smile. If you're sad, you might look down and slouch your shoulders. If you're angry, you might clench your fists and stomp your feet.

Sometimes, people use body language to communicate things that they don't want to say out loud. For example, if someone rolls their eyes or crosses their arms, it might mean that they're annoyed or don't want to talk about something.

It's also great to learn to avoid distractions when you're having a conversation. That means putting away your phone or turning off the TV so you can focus on the person speaking. When you're actively listening, you're not just hearing the words that the person is saying; you're also trying to understand their perspective and feelings.

What are conversational skills?

Good conversation skills include things such as:

- Taking turns speaking
- Asking questions about the other person
- And being respectful by not interrupting

When you take turns speaking, you're giving each person a chance to share their thoughts and feelings. Asking questions shows that you're interested in what the other person is saying and helps you understand their point of view. Being respectful means listening without interrupting, using kind words, and not making fun of what someone is saying.

Using active listening and good conversation skills can help you have better relationships with your family, friends, and teachers. When you're a good listener, people will want to talk to you and share their thoughts and feelings with you. And when you use good conversation skills, you'll be able to express yourself more clearly and have more meaningful conversations with others.

EVERYONE CAN BE HAPPY

It can be hard to share things that we really like or that are special to us, but it's an essential way to show kindness and make friends.

Compromise is another way of sharing. It is finding a solution that works for both you and the other person. It might mean that you have to give up something that you really want in order to make someone else happy, but it's crucial to remember that everyone's needs and wants are important. Compromise is an essential skill that can help you solve problems and build stronger relationships with others.

Remember, compromise is not about winning or losing, it's about finding a solution that everyone can be happy with. So, the next time you have a disagreement with someone, try to find a way to compromise and work together to find a solution that works for everyone involved.

Generosity is another big part of sharing, and it is another awesome social skill. Generosity means being willing to give something to someone else without expecting anything in return. It's like when you offer to share your snack with a friend or help someone with their homework. When you make an effort to share and show generosity, you will build stronger relationships with the people around you. This is because you are showing that you care about them and that you're willing to put their needs before your own sometimes.

So, the next time you're doing something fun, or have something that another person wants to enjoy, remember to practice your sharing skills. You might have to compromise a little or show some generosity, but it will be worth it when you see how happy it makes the people around you!

FOLLOWING DIRECTIONS

Following directions means doing what someone else tells you to do. This is an essential skill that you'll use in school, at home, and later in life as a teenager and adult. To get better at following directions, there are a few great steps you can take, including the following:

1. First, make sure you're paying attention when someone gives you directions. This means looking at the person and listening carefully to what they're saying.
2. It's also to ask questions if you're not sure what someone means or if you need more information. Sometimes, directions can be a little confusing, and it's okay to ask for help.
3. Another important step is to repeat the directions back to the person who gave them to you. This shows that you understand what you're supposed to do and can help you remember the instructions later.
4. Writing down directions that have more steps and things to remember can be a great way of remembering and following more

complicated directions. Sometimes you won't be able to remember everything all on your own, and will need something to look at while you complete the task.

Being able to follow directions can help you be more successful in school and in other areas of your life. For example, when you're doing a group project, it's critical to follow the directions so that everyone is working together and the project is successful. As you get older, following instructions becomes even more necessary. In a job, you'll need to be able to follow directions from your boss or supervisor. In driving, you'll need to follow traffic signs and signals to stay safe on the road.

ENCOURAGING OTHERS

Encouraging others is a really great social skill that can help you build healthy relationships with the people around you. It's all about being supportive and helping others feel good about themselves.

One way to encourage others is to give them compliments. When you notice something good about someone, like their hard work or their kindness, you can tell them how much you appreciate it. This can help boost their confidence and make them feel good about themselves.

Another way to encourage others is to listen to them when they need to talk. Sometimes, all someone needs is a good listener to help them work through a problem or feel better about a situation. By listening and being supportive, you can help others feel valued and cared for.

It's also important to be there for others when they need help. Whether it's helping someone with their homework or offering to carry something heavy, small acts of kindness can go a long way in making someone feel supported and encouraged.

Encouraging others is crucial because it makes other people happy and makes friendships more loving. It can also help to boost your own mood and make you feel good about yourself when you're able to help others.

Remember, encouraging others doesn't have to be complicated. Small acts of kindness and words of support can go a long way in making someone feel valued and cared for.

QUESTIONS FOR YOUR JOURNAL— REFLECTING ON SOCIAL SKILLS

1. Think about someone you admire for their social skills. What can you learn from them?
2. Write about a time when you felt really proud of your social skills. What did you do to make yourself feel that way?
3. Can you think about a time when you practiced compromising? How did you do this? How did you feel and make the other person feel?
4. Write about a time when someone was generous to you. How did it make you feel?
5. Make a list of five things you can do to be more generous to others.
6. Write about a time when you were generous to someone else. How did it make you feel?
7. Write about a time when you had trouble listening to someone else. What was distracting you?
8. Make a list of three things you can do to improve your active listening skills.

9. Write about a time when someone else really listened to you. How did it make you feel

10. Write about a time when you had a really great conversation with someone. What made it so good?

11. Make a list of three conversation topics that you're interested in. Why do these topics interest you?

12. Write about a time when a conversation didn't go as well as you hoped. What could you have done differently?

13. Write about a time when someone encouraged you. How did it make you feel?

14. Make a list of five things you can do to encourage someone else.

15. Write about a time when you encouraged someone else. How did it make you feel?

In conclusion, social skills, generosity, and encouraging others are all big parts of building strong relationships and being a good friend. By practicing these skills, you can improve your ability to get along with others, understand people, and really help your friends.

Next up, we talk all about tips you can use to make more (and better) friends! It can be scary to put yourself out there, but it really doesn't need to be! In the next chapter, you will discover all the tips and strategies to be a better friend.

CHAPTER 3
A GUIDE TO MAKING FRIENDS

Do you know how important it is to have good friends? The people you choose to spend time with can have a big impact on your life, both in good ways and not-so-good ways. That's why you really need to make sure you're surrounding yourself with friends who will make you feel happy and good about yourself, and who will help you be your best self. In this chapter, we're going to talk about how you can make sure you're choosing healthy and supportive friends, and why having good friends (not just a lot of friends) is so helpful for you to feel good and be successful.

WHAT MAKES A GOOD FRIEND?

Making good friends is a big part of growing up. But what makes a good friend? Well, a good friend is someone who is there for you when you need them, who makes you feel happy and supported, and who helps you be the best version of yourself.

So, how can you choose good friends?

One way is to look for people who share your interests and values. If you love soccer, for example, you might want to look for friends who also love playing soccer. If you value honesty and kindness, you might want to look for friends who also value those things.

But making friends is not just about choosing good friends— it's also essential for you to be a good friend as well! Being a good friend means being there for your friends when they need you, listening to them when they want to talk, and treating them with kindness and respect.

Here are some tips for being a good friend:

1. Listen to your friends when they talk to you. Pay attention to what they're saying and how they're feeling.
2. Be supportive of your friends. If they're going through a tough time, offer to help in any way you can.
3. Respect your friends' feelings and opinions, even if they're different from your own.
4. Be honest with your friends. If something is bothering you, talk to them about it in a kind and respectful way.

Remember, friendships take work, but they're worth it! By choosing supportive friends and being a good friend yourself, you can build strong and healthy relationships that will last a lifetime.

CONVERSATIONAL SKILLS— A KEY TO MAKING NEW FRIENDS

Conversational skills are a big part of making friends. When you are able to hold a conversation with others, you are more likely to build strong relationships with those around you. Here are some tips and steps to improve your conversational skills (Homer, 2021):

Practice active listening

When someone is speaking to you, make sure you are fully present and paying attention to the conversation. This means making eye contact, nodding your head, and responding appropriately to what they are saying.

Ask open-ended questions

Instead of asking yes or no questions, try to ask questions that require a more detailed response. This will encourage the other person to share more about themselves and help to keep the conversation going.

Be aware of body language

Your body language can communicate a lot during a conversation. Make sure to maintain good posture, use appropriate gestures, and avoid crossing your arms or legs, which can signal disinterest or defensiveness.

Use appropriate humor

Humor can be a great icebreaker and can help to lighten the mood in any conversation. It can be a great way to connect with new people as well, but it's important to use it appropriately. Avoid making jokes at someone else's expense or using humor to deflect from a serious conversation.

Stay on topic

Try to keep the conversation focused on the topic at hand, and avoid jumping from one topic to another too quickly. This can help to build a more meaningful conversation and make the other person feel heard.

Practice gratitude and appreciation

Showing gratitude can help to build stronger relationships and make others feel appreciated. Make sure to express your appreciation for the other person's time, perspective, and contributions to the conversation.

Share your experiences

When you share your experiences, it can help the other person to get to know you better and also provide a starting point for them to share their own experiences.

Be positive

Being positive can help to make the other person feel more comfortable and can lead to a more enjoyable conversation. Try to avoid complaining or talking negatively about others.

TIPS TO MAKE THE BEST FRIENDS EVER

Making new friends can be really exciting, but it can also feel a little overwhelming. Luckily, there are lots of ways to find and make new friends!

One great way to meet new friends is to get involved in activities or clubs that you enjoy. If you love playing a sport, for example, you might want to join a local team or club. If you love art, you could try taking an art class or joining an art club. This way, you'll be able to meet other kids who share your interests.

Another way to make new friends is to be friendly and approachable. Smile and say hello to people you meet, and be open to talking to new people. You never know who might turn out to be a great friend!

When you're trying to make new friends you also need to remember to be your true self. Don't try to pretend to be someone you're not in order to fit in or impress other people. Your true friends will like you for who you are!

Here are a few more quick ways you can increase your chances of making new friends:

- Volunteer for community programs or charities that you care about.
- Learn a joke! This is a great way to quickly connect with someone and possibly meet a new friend.
- Practice introductions and approaching people. The more you practice talking to new people, the easier it will become.
- Play the "what if" game— This just means asking yourself what the worst thing that could come from something would be. Think about the most ridiculous situations, then figure out if that is even possible. This is a great way to beat anxiety and feel more confident when introducing yourself to new people.
- Make an effort to actively listen when new people are talking to you.
- Ask your parents to introduce you to kids and families they know!
- Be patient— making the best friends who will support you will take time and effort.
- Participate in after-school events and programs! This is a great way to meet kids who are interested in similar things as you… who also go to your school.
- Do things you love! You will naturally meet other people who enjoy doing the same things as you!

Once you've made some new friends, you will need to put effort into building and maintaining those friendships. Make plans to hang out together, whether it's playing a game or going to see a movie. Take the time to listen to your friends when they want to talk, and be there for them when they need your support.

QUESTIONS FOR YOUR JOURNAL— THINKING ABOUT FRIENDSHIPS

1. Think about a time when you made a new friend. How did you start the conversation? What did you talk about? How did you feel afterward?
2. Imagine you're starting a new school or joining a new club. What are some ways you could introduce yourself to others and start making friends?
3. Have you ever felt left out or excluded from a group of friends? How did it make you feel, and what did you do to try to make friends?
4. What qualities do you look for in a friend? Why are these qualities important to you?
5. Think about a time when you had a conflict with a friend. How did you resolve the situation, and what did you learn from it?
6. Have you ever had a friend who moved away or left your school? How did you stay in touch, and what did you do to cope with the change?
7. Imagine you see someone who looks sad or lonely. What could you do to try to make them feel included and welcome?
8. Have you ever had a friend who was different from you in some way (e.g. different race, religion, culture)? How did you learn about their experiences and perspectives, and what did you learn from the friendship?
9. Think about a time when you felt nervous or anxious about meeting new people. What strategies did you use to calm your nerves and make friends?
10. Imagine you're planning a party or event with your friends. What are some ways you could make sure everyone feels included and has a good time?

So, you've learned a lot about making good friends! Remember, it's neccessary to be kind, open-minded, and respectful to others. By being yourself and showing interest in others, you can create strong, lasting friendships.

But what happens when friendships hit a rough patch? What do you do when you and your friend disagree or argue? In the next chapter, we'll talk about how to handle fights and arguments with friends. You'll learn strategies for resolving conflicts and maintaining healthy, positive relationships.

Remember, no friendship is perfect. Everyone has disagreements and misunderstandings from time to time. But with the right tools and mindset, you can work through these challenges and come out even stronger on the other side. So, let's get ready to dive into the next chapter and learn how to handle conflicts with grace and compassion.

CHAPTER 4
HOW TO HANDLE FIGHTS AND ARGUMENTS

At some point, everyone experiences disagreements with their friends, parents, or siblings. Maybe you and your friend have different opinions about something, or perhaps you both want to play a different game. What-ever the reason, disagreements can be tricky to handle, and they can some-times lead to even bigger conflicts.

In this chapter, you will learn how to handle these situations in a healthy and positive way. You'll discover that resolving conflicts with your friends can actually strengthen your friendship and build trust. We'll explore different strategies for resolving disagreements, such as communication, compromise, and empathy. You'll learn how to listen actively, express your feelings respectfully, and find common ground with others. We'll also talk about what to do if you feel like your friend isn't listening or if the disagreement becomes too heated.

HOW TO STOP ARGUMENTS FROM GETTING OUT OF HAND

Sometimes little conflicts can turn into big fights, but there are ways you can stop them from getting out of hand before things go too far. Here are some tips to help you prevent arguments from turning into bigger issues (Garey, 2022):

1. Take a deep breath: When you start to feel frustrated or angry, take a moment to breathe deeply. This can help you calm down and think more clearly.
2. Listen actively: When your friend is talking, listen carefully to what they're saying. Try to understand their point of view, even if you don't agree with it.
3. Express your feelings respectfully: When it's your turn to talk, express your feelings in a calm and respectful way. Use "I" statements to describe how you feel, such as "I feel upset when..." or "I'm frustrated because...".
4. Find common ground: Look for areas of agreement with your friend. Even if you disagree on some things, you might find that you have similar feelings or goals.
5. Take a break: If the argument is getting too heated, suggest taking a break to cool off. You can come back to the conversation later when you're both feeling calmer.

The biggest thing is to handle the situation in a respectful and healthy way. By using these tips, you can prevent arguments from turning into bigger conflicts and keep your friendships strong.

TIPS FOR CONFLICT RESOLUTION

Stopping arguments from becoming worse is a great skill that will help you all throughout your life. But learning how to *resolve* any conflicts you encounter will be just as crucial. Here are a few steps you can take to manage these fights in a healthy way (Garey, 2022):

Think before you speak

When you're in the middle of a conflict, it can be tempting to say the first thing that comes to mind. But taking a moment to think before you speak can help you express yourself more clearly and avoid saying something hurtful. You can ask yourself:

"Do I really mean what I am about to say?"

"Will these words help or hurt the situation?"

"Am I being disrespectful or rude just to prove a point?"

Express yourself clearly

When you're talking with your friend about the conflict, be clear and specific about what's bothering you. Use "I" statements to describe how you feel, such as "I feel upset when you don't listen to me."

When you are able to focus your words on yourself and how you feel, you will be able to express what you need to say in a calmer, less accusatory way. This will also help the other person not feel like they are being attacked.

Compromise

When you're trying to resolve a conflict, you will need to work to find a solution that is good for both you and your friend. Look for areas of agreement and try to find a compromise that meets both of your needs. This doesn't mean that you are "losing" the argument, it just means that both of you get an outcome where you are happy.

Take responsibility

If you've made a mistake or hurt your friend's feelings, it's important to take responsibility for your actions. Apologize sincerely and work to make things right. This shows that you truly care for the other person and are willing to be humble and admit your mistakes.

Here are a couple of examples of how you can use these tips in real-life conflict-resolution situations:

- Imagine you and your friend are arguing over what game to play. You could say, "I understand that you really want to play your game, but I feel upset because we played that game last time. Can we compromise and play a different game this time?"
- Let's say you and your friend are arguing over something more serious, like a misunderstanding that led to hurt feelings. You could say, "I'm sorry if I said something that hurt your feelings. I didn't mean to, and I want to work this out so we can be friends again. Can you help me understand what upset you?"
- Imagine you and your friend are arguing over who gets to use a new game. You could say, "I understand that you want to play with this, but I was using it first. Can we take turns using it instead?"
- Let's say you and your friend are arguing over something you both said during a game. You could say, "I'm sorry if I said something that offended you. I didn't mean to hurt your feelings, and I want to make things right. Can we talk about what happened and figure out a solution?"
- Imagine you and your friend are arguing over a misunderstanding that led to a fight. You could say, "I'm sorry that we got into a fight. I think there was a misunderstanding between us, and I want to clear things up. Can we talk about what happened and try to find a solution together?"

Remember, these conflict resolution tips are just a starting point. Every situation is different, and it's essential to be flexible and open-minded when trying to work through a conflict with a friend. With practice, you'll get better at resolving conflicts in a healthy and respectful way, and your friendships will be stronger as a result.

PRACTICING RESPECT— IT'S NOT JUST FOR ADULTS

Respect is a really big part of managing fights and arguments, and it's something that everyone can practice, no matter how old they are. Here's why respect is such a great skill to learn:

Respect helps you understand other people's perspectives

When you're in an argument or a fight with someone, it's easy to get caught up in your own feelings and opinions. But if you show respect for the other person and their perspective, you're more likely to be able to see the situation from their point of view. This can help you come up with a solution that works for both of you.

Respect makes it easier to communicate

When you're respectful toward the other person, it creates a more positive atmosphere for communication. This means that you're more likely to be able to express your feelings and opinions clearly, and the other person is more likely to listen to what you have to say.

Respect helps you build stronger relationships: When you show respect for the other person, it helps to build trust and mutual understanding. This can lead to stronger and more meaningful relationships, even if you've had disagreements in the past.

Respect shows that you value the other person

When you're respectful toward the other person, it shows that you value them as a person, even if you don't agree with everything they say or do. This can help to create a more positive and constructive relationship, even when you're dealing with difficult situations.

Here are a few examples of ways you can show your respect to the people around you:

1. Listen to others when they speak, without interrupting or talking over them.
2. Use kind and polite words when speaking to others, like "please" and "thank you."
3. Avoid name-calling or saying hurtful things to others, even when you're angry.
4. Be open-minded and willing to consider other people's opinions, even if you don't agree with them.
5. Treat others the way you would want to be treated, with kindness and fairness.
6. Be patient and understanding when others make mistakes or don't understand something.
7. Respect other people's personal space and belongings.
8. Show appreciation and gratitude for the people in your life, like your parents, teachers, or friends.
9. Offer to help others when they need it, like holding the door open or carrying something heavy.
10. Stand up for others who are being treated unfairly or bullied, and show empathy and understanding toward them.

Remember, respect is a two-way street. If you want others to show you respect, you need to show them respect as well. This means listening to their opinions, speaking to them in a kind and respectful way, and being willing to compromise and work together to find solutions to problems. By practicing respect in all of your relationships, you'll be able to manage fights and arguments in a healthier and more positive way.

QUESTIONS FOR YOUR JOURNAL— REFLECTING ON CONFLICTS

1. Describe a time when you had to resolve a conflict with a friend. What did you do to resolve the conflict, and how did it make you feel?

2. Think about a time when you had to compromise with someone. How did you come to a compromise, and how did it affect your relationship with that person?
3. Write about a situation where you felt disrespected by someone. How did you handle it, and what could you have done differently?
4. Describe a time when you showed respect toward someone, even if you didn't agree with them. What did you do, and how did it make the other person feel?
5. Think about a time when you had to apologize to someone. How did you approach the situation, and what did you learn from it?
6. Write about a time when you felt misunderstood by someone. How did you communicate your feelings, and what could you have done differently to avoid the misunderstanding?
7. Describe a situation where you had to work together with someone to achieve a goal. How did you work together, and what did you learn about compromise and collaboration?
8. Think about a time when you had to stand up for someone who was being treated unfairly. What did you do, and how did it make you feel?
9. Write about a situation where you had to use your problem-solving skills to resolve a conflict. What steps did you take, and what was the outcome?
10. Describe a time when you felt really proud of yourself for resolving a conflict in a positive way. What did you do, and how did it make you feel about yourself and your relationships with others?

Conflict resolution practices are essential life skills that can help you build stronger and more positive relationships with the people around you. By learning to communicate effectively, compromise when necessary, and show respect toward others, you can create a more peaceful and harmonious environment for yourself and those around you.

In the next chapter, we will be discussing another heavy topic that many kids face: peer pressure. This can come in many forms and can be difficult to navigate, but by understanding how to make healthy choices and stand up for yourself, you can learn to resist bad influences and make choices that align with what you believe We will explore strategies for handling peer pressure and developing the confidence and strength to stay true to yourself, even in challenging situations.

CHAPTER 5
PEER PRESSURE

Peers are people who are about the same age as you and who share similar experiences, interests, and backgrounds. In other words, your peers are kids who are in the same grade, class, or school as you. Peers can be friends, classmates, teammates, or anyone else who you spend time with and share things in common with. It's necessary to have positive peer relationships because they can provide support, encouragement, and friendship.

As you grow up, you may start to feel pressure from your friends or peers to do things that you might not be comfortable with or that go against your values. This is what we call peer pressure.

Peer pressure can feel overwhelming and can make you feel like you have to do something just to fit in or be accepted by your peers. It can come in many forms, like feeling pressured to dress a certain way, do certain things, talk in a different way, or participate in other risky behaviors.

While it's normal to want to fit in and be liked by others, peer pressure can be harmful if it leads you to make choices that go against your values or that put your health and well-being at risk. That's why you will need to learn how to identify and resist negative influences from your peers, and make choices that align with your own beliefs and goals.

In this chapter, we will explore the different types of peer pressure, how it manifests, and why it can be harmful. We will also provide you with tips and strategies for handling peer pressure in a healthy and positive way, so that you can stay true to yourself and make choices that are right for you. So, let's dive in and learn more about peer pressure together!

WHAT DOES PEER PRESSURE LOOK AND FEEL LIKE?

There are many different kinds of peer pressure that you might experience as a kid or a teenager. Here are a few common types of peer pressure and what they might look like (GreatSchools, 2022):

Direct Peer Pressure

This is when someone asks you to do something you don't want to do. For example, a friend might ask you to wear something different, or do something with them that you don't agree with. In this case, you might feel like you have to do what your friend is asking so that you don't upset them or so that they'll like you more. But remember, it's important to think about the consequences of your actions and to make your own decisions based on what you believe is right.

Indirect Peer Pressure

This is when someone tries to influence you to do something without directly asking you. For example, your friends might talk about how cool it is to not do your homework or be rude to your teacher, making you feel like you should do it too. In this case, you will need to remember that you don't have to go along with what your friends are saying. You can choose to do what's best for you, even if it's different from what your friends are doing.

Positive Peer Pressure

This is when your friends encourage you to do something good, like join a club or help others. For example, your friend might invite you to volunteer at a charity event. This type of peer pressure can be a good thing, as it can help you to try new things and make positive changes in your life. Just remember to always make your own choices and do what feels right for you.

Negative Peer Pressure

This is when your friends encourage you to do something bad, like bully someone or steal something. For example, your friends might tease you for not wanting to shoplift, making you feel like you should do it to fit in. This type of peer pressure is always wrong and can lead to negative consequences. If you ever feel pressured to do something that goes against your values, it's important to stand up for yourself and say no.

Remember, you always have the power to make your own decisions and to choose what's best for you. By learning about the different types of peer pressure and how to handle them, you can feel more confident in your ability to stand up for yourself and make positive choices.

TIPS FOR HANDLING PEER PRESSURE

Now that you know about what peer pressure can look and feel like, it's time to discover some real tips and steps you can follow to deal with peer pressure (GreatSchools, 2022).

1. Talk to a parent: If you're feeling pressured by your friends, it can be helpful to talk to a parent or another trusted adult about what's going on. They can offer you support and guidance and help you to make the best decision for yourself.
2. Be prepared with an escape or excuse: If you know that you'll be in a situation where you might feel pressured, it's a good idea to have an escape plan or an excuse ready. For example, if your friends are planning to skip school, you can say that you have a doctor's appointment or a family obligation.
3. Have code words with parents who can get you out of uncomfortable situations: This can be a great way for you to let a parent know that something is wrong without showing the people around you that you want to leave. For example, if you call your mom and say "pineapple," she knows that you need her to come pick you up right away.
4. Be confident in your decisions: It's important to be confident in the decisions you make, even if they're different from what your friends are doing. Remember, you have the right to say no and to do what feels right for you.
5. Surround yourself with positive influences: Finally, surrounding yourself with positive influences will be crucial. Spend time with friends who share your values and who support you in making good choices.
6. Practice saying no: One of the best ways to handle peer pressure is to practice saying no in advance. You can practice in front of a mirror or with a friend, and come up with different ways to say no without being confrontational.
7. Find alternatives: If your friends are pressuring you to do something that you're uncomfortable with, try suggesting alternative activities that you'd all enjoy. For example, if your

friends want to smoke, you can suggest going to the park or playing a game instead.

8. Avoid situations where you're likely to feel pressured: If you know that a certain group of friends or a certain situation is likely to result in peer pressure, try to avoid those situations as much as possible.

9. Take a break: Sometimes, all you need is a break from the situation to gain some perspective. If you're feeling pressured, try taking a walk or finding a quiet place to clear your head.

Handling peer pressure can be challenging, but by following these tips, you can feel more confident in your ability to make your own choices and to stand up for yourself. Also remember that it may take time for others to respect where you stand and draw your lines, and that is okay. You are stronger than you know. You've got this!

QUESTIONS FOR YOUR JOURNAL— THINKING ABOUT PEER PRESSURE

1. Describe a time when you experienced peer pressure. How did you handle it? What did you learn from the experience?
2. Have you ever experienced positive peer pressure? Describe a time when your friends encouraged you to do something positive, like joining a sports team or volunteering for a community project.
3. What are some common situations where you might feel peer pressure? How can you prepare yourself to handle these situations?
4. Think of a time when you saw someone else being pressured by their peers. What could you have done to help?
5. Have you ever given in to peer pressure even though you didn't want to? How did you feel afterward?
6. What are some strategies you are going to start using to say no to peer pressure?
7. How can you support a friend who is facing peer pressure? What can you do to help them feel more confident and supported?
8. Think of a time when you stood up to peer pressure and said no. How did you feel afterward? What did you learn from the experience?

Dealing with peer pressure is rarely easy, but it is important to remember that you have the power to make your own choices. By using the tips and strategies we've discussed in this chapter, you can better navigate peer pressure situations and stay true to yourself.

In the next chapter, we'll be talking about empathy–the ability to understand and share the feelings of others. Understanding empathy can help you be a better friend and a more compassionate person.

CHAPTER 6
WHAT IS EMPATHY?

Empathy is the ability to understand and share the feelings of others. It involves being able to put yourself in someone else's shoes and understand their perspective.

Empathy is beneficial because it helps you build stronger relationships with others. When you can understand how someone is feeling, you can respond in a way that is more supportive and helpful. This can help you become a better friend and improve your social skills.

Being empathetic can also help you better understand and manage your own emotions. When you are able to recognize and understand the emotions of others, you may become more aware of your own emotions and learn how to manage them more effectively.

So, what does empathy feel like? When you are being empathetic, you may feel a sense of connection with the person you are talking to. You may feel their emotions as if they were your own, which can be both rewarding and challenging. Empathy requires that you are willing to be vulnerable and open to the emotions of others, which can be difficult at times.

What does empathy look like in action? It can take many forms, such as listening attentively, offering support, or simply being present for someone in need. Empathy can also involve showing kindness and understanding to others, even when you don't agree with them.

In this chapter, we will explore empathy in more depth! You will also learn how to develop and practice empathy in your own life. Let's jump right in!

EMPATHY IN DAILY LIFE

Empathy is an essential quality that can help you become a better person and build stronger relationships with others. As you approach your teenage years, empathy becomes even more important as you get into complicated social situations and learn more about what's happening in the world. By practicing empathy in your daily life, you can become a more kind, caring, and understanding person, which will benefit you and those around you in countless ways.

So, what does empathy look like in daily life? Here are some examples (Williamson, 2021):

1. Listening: One of the biggest ways of showing empathy is by actively listening to others. When someone is talking to you, try to focus on what they are saying and give them your full attention. This shows that you value their thoughts and feelings.

2. Understanding: Empathy involves understanding how others are feeling, even if you haven't experienced the same thing yourself. Try to put yourself in their shoes and imagine what it would be like to be in their situation.

3. Support: Showing support to someone who is going through a difficult time is a powerful way to show empathy. This could involve offering words of encouragement, giving a comforting hug, or simply being there for them when they need it.

4. Kindness: Small acts of kindness can go a long way in showing empathy. This could include offering to help with a task, bringing someone a thoughtful gift, or doing something nice for them just because.

5. Respect: Empathy involves showing respect to others, even if you disagree with them. This could involve listening to their point of view, being open-minded, and treating them with kindness and compassion.

But how can you actually take steps to become a more empathetic person? The next section is all about small things you can do to practice empathy every day!

STEPS TO DEVELOP EMPATHY

Developing empathy, and practicing it, will be a process that you need to continue exercising through the rest of your life. It takes effort and dedication, so keep these steps and practices in mind when you are looking to become more empathetic (Williamson, 2021):

- Put yourself in someone else's shoes: When you're interacting with others, try to imagine what it might feel like to be in their situation. For example, if someone is upset, try to imagine how you would feel if you were in their shoes.
- Ask questions: Ask questions about other people's experiences, feelings, and opinions. This will help you better understand their perspective and build empathy toward them.

- Practice compassion: Show compassion to others by offering help or kind words. This will help you to develop a greater understanding of what it's like to be in someone else's shoes.
- Show interest in others: Make an effort to learn about others' hobbies, interests, and passions. This will not only help you to build stronger relationships, but also increase your understanding of others.
- Volunteer and help others: Volunteering and helping others is a great way to develop empathy. By helping those in need, you'll gain a better understanding of their struggles and challenges.
- Practice random acts of kindness: Do something nice for someone without expecting anything in return. This can be as simple as holding the door open or offering a compliment. It will help you develop a sense of empathy and kindness toward others.

- Learn about different cultures: Understanding different cultures can help you become more open-minded and empathetic toward others who may have different beliefs, customs, or backgrounds.

- Watch movies and read books: By reading or watching things with different perspectives and experiences you will effectively exercise your empathy muscle. This will help you understand others better and expand your empathy.
- Role-play: Practice putting yourself in different scenarios and imagining how you would react if you were in someone else's situation. This can help you develop your empathy skills.
- Talk to someone different from you: Strike up a conversation with someone you wouldn't normally talk to, such as a new student at school or someone from a different grade. This will help you understand different perspectives and develop empathy toward others.

EMPATHY AND FORGIVENESS

Forgiveness and empathy both play big parts when it comes to being a kind and understanding person. Let's talk about how they are connected and how you can practice forgiveness.

You already know that empathy is about trying to understand how someone else is feeling. It helps us connect with others and be there for them when they need us.

Forgiveness, on the other hand, is when you choose to let go of anger or resentment toward someone who has hurt you. Forgiving someone can be really hard, but it's an essential part of being a good friend and family member. Here are a few other reasons why forgiveness is so important:

- It can help you feel better: When someone hurts you, it can be really hard to let go of those feelings of anger and sadness. But, holding onto those negative emotions can make you feel even worse. Forgiving someone can help you feel lighter and less weighed down by negative feelings.
- It can improve your relationships: When you forgive someone, it can help to repair a damaged relationship. By letting go of anger and resentment, you can create a more positive and healthy relationship with the person who hurt you.

- It can help you grow and learn: Forgiveness can be a really powerful tool for personal growth. By choosing to forgive someone, you are showing that you are able to understand their perspective and work to make things better for both of you.
- It can make the world a better place: Forgiveness is all about kindness and understanding. By practicing forgiveness, you are spreading positivity and helping to create a more peaceful world.

Here are a few steps you can take to practice forgiveness:

1. Take a deep breath: When someone hurts you, it can be really upsetting. Take a deep breath and try to calm down before you react.
2. Think about why they did it: Sometimes people make mistakes because they are going through a tough time or because they don't know any better. Try to understand why they did what they did.
3. Talk to them: If you feel comfortable, talk to the person who hurt you and let them know how you feel. Maybe they didn't even realize they hurt you and can apologize.
4. Let it go: Once you've talked it out and tried to understand their perspective, it's time to let it go. Holding onto anger and resentment will only hurt you in the long run.

QUESTIONS FOR YOUR JOURNAL— THINKING ABOUT EMPATHY

1. Imagine you saw someone crying at school. How would you feel? What would you do to try to make them feel better?
2. Think about a time when someone helped you when you were feeling sad. How did their kindness make you feel? How can you show kindness to others when they are feeling down?
3. Imagine you accidentally hurt someone's feelings. How would you feel? What could you do to make things right?
4. Think about a time when someone was kind to you even though you didn't know them well. How did that make you feel? How can you show kindness to strangers?

5. Imagine you saw someone being bullied. How would you feel? What could you do to help them?
6. Think about a time when you had to apologize to someone. How did you feel? What did you learn from the experience?
7. Imagine you were in someone else's shoes. How would you feel? What would you want others to do to help you?
8. Think about a time when you were able to help someone else. How did that make you feel? How can you continue to help others?
9. Imagine you saw someone who was different from you. How would you feel? What could you do to learn more about their culture or background?
10. Think about a time when you made a mistake and someone forgave you. How did that make you feel? How can you show forgiveness to others?

Let's move on to talking about something a lot of kids dread… school. Whether you struggle with friends, tough teachers, or hard homework assignments, the next chapter will help you out. We'll cover everything you need to know in order to make your school experience more pleasant.

CHAPTER 7
TIPS FOR SCHOOL

In this chapter, we'll explore some essential skills that will help you thrive in school. As a student, you spend a lot of time at school, so life will be easier if you develop the skills that help you succeed there. Whether you're in elementary or middle school, these are skills that will pay off for the rest of your life. From organizing your work to being a good listener, you'll learn valuable strategies that will help you excel in your studies and make the most out of your school experience. So get ready to boost your school skills and become a superstar student!

Why is school even important?

Have you ever wondered why you have to go to school every day? It might seem like a lot of work and not very fun, but school is incredibly necessary for your future.

First of all, school teaches you amazing skills that you will need throughout your life. You learn how to read, write, and do math, which are essential for almost any job you might want in the future. You also learn how to solve problems, work with others, and think critically. These skills will help you in everything from your personal relationships to your career.

In addition to teaching you valuable skills, school helps you explore your interests and passions. You get to learn about different subjects like history, science, and art, and you might discover something that really interests you. This can help you figure out what you want to do when you grow up and what kind of career you want to have.

Another big reason why school is so essential is that it helps you build a strong foundation for your future. The knowledge and skills you learn in school will prepare you for college or other education after high school, which can open up even more opportunities for you in the future.

Finally, school helps you learn how to be a grown-up so you'll be ready to live your own life when you're old enough. You learn things like hard work, responsibility, and respect, and you have the opportunity to practice them every day in your classes and interactions with others.

So, as you can see, school is a key to your future. Even though it might not always be easy or fun, remember that every day you spend learning is an investment in your future success.

DEALING WITH SCHOOL ANXIETY

Do you ever feel nervous about going to school? It's okay if you do—school anxiety is a common feeling that many students experience. So, here is what you need to know about school anxiety and some tips on how to overcome it (Morin, 2021).

School anxiety is a feeling of worry or fear that you might have about going to school. This feeling can be caused by many things, such as a fear of not doing well in school, being afraid of people not liking you, or even just feeling overwhelmed by the amount of work you have to do.

One way to overcome school anxiety is to talk to someone about it. You can talk to your parents, your teacher, or even a school counselor. They can help you understand why you're feeling anxious and give you tips on how to cope with it.

Another way to overcome school anxiety is to be prepared. Make sure you have all the supplies you need for class, and try to organize your work so that you feel less overwhelmed. You can also make a schedule to help you manage your time better and reduce stress.

It's also important to take care of yourself when you're feeling anxious. Make sure you're getting enough sleep, eating healthy foods, and exercising regularly. These things can help you feel better physically and mentally, which can reduce your anxiety.

Lastly, try to focus on the positives of going to school. Think about the things you enjoy doing in school, like seeing your friends or learning about a subject you like. By focusing on the things you enjoy, you can reduce your anxiety and make school a more positive experience.

TIPS FOR MAKING ALLIES WITH YOUR TEACHERS

Have you ever thought about becoming friends with your teachers? While they are there to teach you, they can also become your allies and help you succeed even more in school. Below are some reasons why you should actually try to be friends with your teachers as well as some steps you can take to get on their good side.

First of all, your teachers want you to succeed! They are there to help you learn and grow, and they want you to do well in school. By becoming friends with them, you can build a positive relationship with them that can help you in many ways. In fact, the more open you are to their help and partnership, the more open they will be to supporting you in different ways!

One way to make allies with your teachers is to show them that you are interested in learning. Ask questions in class, participate in discussions, and show them that you care about your education. You can also show them respect by listening attentively and following their instructions.

Another way to make allies with your teachers is to show them that you are responsible and reliable. Turn in your homework on time, come to class prepared, and be respectful to your classmates. By doing these things, your teachers will see that you are a responsible and trustworthy student, and they will be more likely to help you out when you need it.

Lastly, don't be afraid to talk to your teachers outside of class. You can ask them for advice, talk to them about your goals, or just chat about your interests. By doing this, you can build a stronger relationship with them and show them that you are interested in their lives as well.

ORGANIZATIONAL AND STUDY TIPS

Going to school can be a lot of work, but there are ways to make it easier. Here are some organizational and study tips to help you succeed in school.

First, let's talk about organization. One way to stay organized is to use a planner or calendar to keep track of your assignments and due dates. Write down all of your homework, projects, and tests, and make sure to check your planner regularly so that you don't forget anything.

A different way you can stay organized is to keep your school supplies in order. Make sure you have all the supplies you need for class, and keep them in a place where you can easily find them. This will help you avoid the stress of not being able to find what you need when you need it.

Here are a few quick tips to keep your things nice and organized:

1. Use a pencil case: A pencil case is a great way to keep all of your writing utensils in one place. Make sure it's big enough to hold all of your pens, pencils, highlighters, and markers, and keep it in your backpack or desk so that you always know where to find it.
2. Keep a folder for each subject: Use different colored folders to keep your notes, handouts, and assignments organized by subject. Label each folder with the name of the subject and keep them in a binder or folder holder.
3. Use dividers: If you have a binder, use dividers to separate different sections, like notes, handouts, and homework. This will make it easier to find what you need and keep everything in order.
4. Label everything: Label all of your notebooks, folders, and binders with your name and the subject. This will make it easier to identify your things if you misplace them, and it can help you stay organized.
5. Clean out your backpack regularly: Make a habit of cleaning out your backpack once a week. Throw away any trash, recycle old papers, and make sure all of your school supplies are where they

belong. This will help you stay organized and avoid clutter in your backpack.

When it comes to studying, there are many different tips you can use. One helpful tip is to take breaks while you study. Studying for long periods of time can be tiring and make it hard to focus. Take short breaks to rest your brain and come back to studying feeling refreshed.

Another study tip is to make flashcards. Flashcards are a great way to memorize information, like vocabulary words or historical dates. You can make them easily and use them to quiz yourself or study with a friend.

Lastly, make sure to stay on top of your assignments. Don't wait until the last minute to start a project or study for a test. Give yourself plenty of time to complete your work, and ask for help if you need it. Your teachers and parents are there to help you, so don't be afraid to ask for assistance. Here are a few additional tips to keep yourself on top of your school work:

1. Keep a planner or a to-do list: Write down all your assignments, homework, and upcoming projects in a planner or to-do list. This will help you stay organized and ensure that you don't forget any important deadlines.

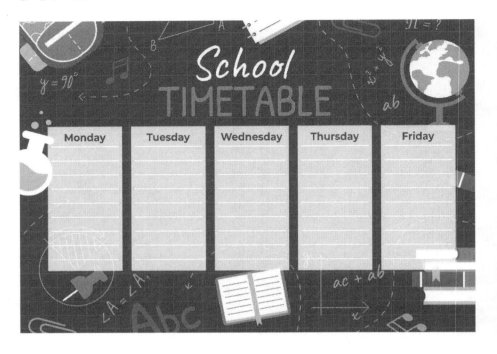

2. Break down larger projects into smaller tasks: If you have a large project or assignment, break it down into smaller, manageable tasks. This will make it less overwhelming and help you make progress each day.

3. Set aside a specific time each day for homework: Set aside a specific time each day to work on your assignments. This will help you establish a routine and ensure that you have enough time to complete your work.

4. Start early: Don't wait until the last minute to start your assignments. The earlier you start, the more time you have to complete them and the less stressed you'll be.

5. Stay focused: When you're working on your assignments, try to eliminate distractions like your phone or social media. This will help you stay focused and get your work done more efficiently.

Taking notes is another great way to remember, and be able to look back on, what you learned. Below are some tips to help you out:

1. Be organized: Use a notebook or binder to keep all your notes in one place. This will make it easier to find what you need later on.
2. Listen actively: Pay attention to what your teacher is saying and try to identify the main ideas and key points.
3. Use abbreviations: Develop your own system of abbreviations and symbols to help you write more quickly.
4. Write in your own words: Try to paraphrase what your teacher is saying in your own words. This will help you understand the material better and remember it more easily.
5. Use headings and bullet points: Use headings and bullet points to organize your notes and make them easier to read.
6. Highlight the most important information: Use a highlighter to mark the key information that you want to remember or study later on.
7. Review your notes: Take some time after class to review your notes and make sure you understand the material. If you have any questions, ask your teacher for clarification.

Remember, effective note-taking is a skill that takes practice. Keep working at it and you'll soon find a system that works best for you!

QUESTIONS FOR YOUR JOURNAL— THINKING ABOUT SCHOOL MORE POSITIVELY

1. What is your favorite subject in school? Why do you enjoy it?
2. Have you ever made friends with one of your teachers? If so, how did you do it?
3. How do you stay organized when you have multiple assignments to complete?
4. Do you prefer to study alone or with a group? Why?
5. What are some strategies you use to remember important information?
6. How do you handle stress when you have a lot of schoolwork to do?
7. Have you ever participated in a school club or activity? If so, which one and what did you enjoy about it?
8. What do you think makes a good teacher? Why?

9. Do you have a favorite study spot or location where you like to do your homework? If so, where is it and why do you like it?
10. What is something you have learned recently in school that you found interesting or exciting? Why did you enjoy it?

School doesn't need to be a bad or scary experience, and the above tips and tricks can really help make it a lot more positive. You have the power to make the most of your school days, be organized, and make friends with your teachers—it just takes some time and effort.

In the next chapter, you will discover more ways to overcome nervousness, this time when it comes to talking to adults!

CHAPTER 8
HOW TO TALK TO ADULTS

Do you ever feel nervous when you need to talk to an adult? Are you worried that they won't listen to you or that your ideas and thoughts aren't important enough to them? The truth is, most adults do want to hear from you and value your opinions.

It's natural to feel a little intimidated by grown-ups who seem to have all the answers, but remember that they were kids once too. They may not always have the right solution, but they are often willing to help and guide you.

Talking to adults can be a valuable way to get advice, share your thoughts and feelings, and even make new connections. Whether it's a teacher, a parent, or a family friend, there are people in your life who want to support you and help you grow.

In this chapter, we'll explore some tips for talking to adults with confidence and ease. You'll learn how to express yourself clearly, listen actively, and build strong relationships with the adults in your life. So, don't be afraid to speak up and share your ideas— you might be surprised at how much you have to offer!

THE POWER OF INTRODUCTIONS AND FIRST IMPRESSIONS

When talking to adults, it's good to try to make a good first impression because this can shape how they view you and how they interact with you in the future. Introductions are a big part of this process because they allow you to start off on the right foot.

Why are first impressions and introductions so important?

Imagine if you met someone for the first time and they didn't introduce themselves or say hello. You might feel confused or even a bit put off. On the other hand, if someone introduces themselves with a smile and a friendly greeting, you'll likely feel more at ease and open to talking with them.

To make a good introduction, start with a smile and a friendly tone of voice. Say hello and introduce yourself by saying your name. You can also add a little bit of information about yourself, like your age or where you're from. For example, "Hi, I'm Sarah and I'm ten years old. Nice to meet you!"

It's also essential to listen carefully to the other person's name and use it when you talk to them. This shows that you're paying attention and that you value their presence.

Remember, first impressions can be *lasting* impressions, so make sure to present yourself in a positive and respectful way. This means being polite, making eye contact, and speaking clearly. Avoid interrupting the other person or fidgeting with your phone or other distractions.

"Hi, my name is Jack and I'm ten years old. It's nice to meet you! What's your name?"

And here's an example of a not-so-good introduction:

"Hey, what's up? I'm like, totally bored. What's your name?"

By making a good first impression and introducing yourself properly, you'll set the stage for a positive and respectful conversation with the adults in your life.

Here are a few more ways you can make an amazing first impression with the people around you (including adults!):

1. Smile and be friendly: When you meet someone new, give them a smile and a warm greeting. This will help them feel comfortable around you and show that you are happy to meet them.
2. Use good manners: Saying "please" and "thank you" and being polite can go a long way in making a good impression. This shows that you are respectful and considerate of others.

3. Make eye contact: When you are speaking with someone, try to look them in the eyes. This shows that you are paying attention to what they are saying and that you are interested in the conversation.

4. Dress appropriately: Dressing appropriately for the occasion can help you make a good impression. If you're not sure what to wear, ask your parents or a trusted adult for advice.

5. Be yourself: It's important to be true to yourself and not try to be someone you're not. People appreciate authenticity and honesty.

6. Listen actively: When someone is speaking to you, listen carefully and ask questions if you don't understand something. This shows that you are interested in what they are saying and that you respect their opinions.

7. Show confidence: Standing up straight, speaking clearly, and making eye contact can help you appear confident and self-assured. This can help you make a good impression on others.

WHAT YOUR BODY LANGUAGE IS TELLING THE WORLD

When you're talking to adults, it's not just about what you say, but also how you say it. Your body language can say a lot about you and can affect how the adult perceives you. Here are some tips on using body language to talk to adults in a confident way:

1. Stand up straight: When you stand up straight, it shows that you are confident and self-assured. It also makes you appear taller and more powerful, which can help you feel more confident.

2. Make eye contact: Making eye contact shows that you are interested in what the adult is saying and that you are paying attention. It also shows that you are confident and respectful.

3. Use open body language: This means not crossing your arms or legs, which can make you appear closed off and unapproachable. Instead, try to keep your arms and legs uncrossed and your hands relaxed at your sides.

4. Smile: Smiling can help you appear friendly and approachable. It also shows that you are confident and happy to be talking to an adult.

5. Nod your head: Nodding your head can show that you are listening and that you understand what the adult is saying. It can also encourage them to keep talking.

On the other hand, there are some body language cues that can make you appear nervous or uncomfortable, such as playing with your hair or clothes, avoiding eye contact, or slouching. If you see yourself doing these things, try to relax and use some of the confident body language tips above.

Your body language can say a lot about you and can affect what others think about you. By using confident body language when talking to adults, you can show them that you are respectful, interested, and self-assured.

MORE TIPS FOR HAVING A CONVERSATION WITH AN ADULT

Here are a few more ways you can get better at holding conversations with adults (and make yourself less nervous):

1. Take a deep breath: Before you start the conversation, take a deep breath to help calm your nerves.
2. Practice what you want to say: If you're nervous, it can be helpful to practice what you want to say beforehand.
3. Ask questions: Asking the adult questions about themselves or their interests can help take the pressure off of you and can also show that you are interested in getting to know them.
4. Listen carefully: Listen carefully to what the adult is saying and ask follow-up questions to show that you are paying attention.
5. Take turns talking: Don't interrupt the adult when they are speaking. Instead, wait for them to finish before responding.
6. Be respectful: Use good manners and be respectful when talking to an adult. This shows that you are polite and considerate.
7. Find common ground: Look for things that you and the adult have in common, such as shared interests or hobbies.
8. Be yourself: It's important to be true to yourself and not try to be someone you're not. People appreciate authenticity and honesty.

9. Don't be afraid to ask what something means: If you don't understand something the adult is saying, don't be afraid to ask what the words they said mean.
10. Take your time: Don't rush the conversation. Take your time and speak at a comfortable pace.
11. Use positive body language: Make eye contact, nod your head, and smile to show that you care about the conversation.

Remember, adults are people who were kids in the past too! They probably had the same nervousness that you have. By following the tips and strategies in this chapter, you can get over being scared and have a great conversation with an adult!

Coming up, we will discover what bullying really is, how to recognize it, what to do if you or someone else is being bullied, and more!

CHAPTER 9
WHAT IS BULLYING?

Bullying is when someone is mean to you over and over again. It can happen in lots of different ways. Sometimes, someone might call you mean names or make fun of you. Other times, they might hurt you physically by pushing or hitting you.

Bullying can come in different forms, and it's important to know what they are so you can recognize them if they happen to you or someone you know.

One type of bullying is called verbal bullying. This is when someone uses words to hurt you. They might call you mean names, make fun of you, or say things that make you feel bad about yourself. Verbal bullying can happen in person, but it can also happen online or through text messages.

Another type of bullying is called physical bullying. This is when someone uses their body to hurt you. They might push you, hit you, or kick you. Physical bullying can be really scary and it can hurt a lot.

A third type of bullying is called social bullying. This is when someone tries to hurt you by making you feel left out or alone. They might spread rumors about you or tell other people not to be your friend. Social bullying can be really hurtful because it makes you feel like nobody likes you.

Bullying can be really dangerous for both the bully and the victim. When someone bullies others, they might think they're just joking around, but they can hurt people's feelings and make them feel really sad or angry. This can lead to problems in school or at home, and even cause depression or anxiety.

For the victim, being bullied can be really scary and stressful. It can make you feel like you don't belong or that something is wrong with you. This can lead to low self-esteem and make it harder to make friends or enjoy things you used to like.

Did You Know… It's Cool to be Nice!

If someone is bullying you, it can be really scary and stressful. But you need to remember that you don't have to face it alone. Here are some things you can do if you're being bullied:

- Stay calm: It can be hard to stay calm when someone is being mean to you, but try to take a deep breath and remember that their words or actions are not your fault.
- Get away: If you are being bullied with words, actions, or online messages a big first step is to get away from it. Find a way to shut off your computer, block them, or leave the room. If it is in person, try and get across the room or into a separate room. This space will give you some protection and comfort.
- Speak up: If you feel safe, try to tell the person who is bullying you that what they're doing is not okay. You can say something like, "Stop, you're hurting my feelings," or "That's not funny; please don't do that."
- Get help: It's essential to tell an adult you trust, like a teacher or parent, if you're being bullied. They can help you come up with a plan to deal with the bullying and make sure you feel safe.

It's also necessary to remember that you can be a role model for kindness and show others that it's cool to be nice. Here are some things you can do to be a good friend and prevent bullying:

- Treat others with kindness and respect: Be a good listener, show empathy, and try to understand how others are feeling.
- Don't bully back: Even if you're angry or upset, don't try to get revenge by bullying the person who hurt you. This will only make things worse.
- Stand up for others: If you see someone being bullied, try to help them. You can say something like "Hey, that's not cool. Leave them alone."

By being kind and standing up for what's right, you can make a difference in the world and show others that it's cool to be nice. Remember, everyone deserves to be treated with respect, and you have the power to make a positive impact on the people around you.

TALKING ABOUT IT

If you are being bullied in any way, let an adult know. This way they can help you figure out the situation, give you advice, and help out in other ways. Here are a few tips for opening up to an adult if you are being bullied:

1. Find an adult you trust: You will need to talk to an adult you feel comfortable with and who you know will take you seriously. This could be a parent, teacher, coach, or school counselor.
2. Be honest: When you talk to an adult, be honest about what's happening to you. Tell them exactly what the bully is doing and how it's making you feel.
3. Ask for help: Let the adult know that you need their help to deal with the bullying. Ask them what they can do to help you feel safe and supported.
4. Provide details: Try to give as much information as possible about the bullying. This can include when and where it's happening, who is involved, and any witnesses who may have seen what's happening.
5. Follow up: After you talk to the adult, make sure to follow up with them and let them know if the bullying continues. They can help you come up with a plan to deal with it and make sure you feel safe.

Remember to speak up if you're being bullied. You don't have to face it alone, and there are people who can help you. By talking to an adult and asking for their help, you're taking a big step toward ending the bullying and feeling safe and supported.

WHAT TO DO IF YOU SEE SOMEONE ELSE BEING BULLIED

Bullying is never okay, even if it is not hurting you directly. If you see someone else being bullied, here are a few different things you can do (Garey, 2022):

1. Check if it's safe: Before doing anything, make sure that you're not in danger. If someone is getting hurt physically, get help from an adult.
2. Speak up: If it's safe, tell the bully to stop. You can say things like, "That's not nice," or "Leave them alone." This shows the person being bullied that you're on their side.

3. Support the person being bullied: After speaking up, let the person being bullied know that you're there for them. You can offer to walk with them or sit with them during lunch.

4. Get help: If the bullying continues, tell an adult you trust. This can be a teacher, coach, or parent. They can help make sure the person being bullied is safe and stop the bullying from happening again.

5. Don't join in: Even if other people are laughing or encouraging the bullying, don't join in. It's essential to *show* that you don't support bullying and that it's not okay.

6. Be kind: Be kind to the person being bullied. You can offer a compliment or a smile to show that they are valued and appreciated.

7. Be a good listener: If the person being bullied wants to talk, be a good listener. Let them know that you hear them and that their feelings matter.

8. Help the person being bullied find support: If the person being bullied is struggling, help them find support. This could be talking to a teacher or counselor, or finding a group or club where they can make new friends.

9. Be a role model: By being kind and standing up for what's right, you can be a role model for others. Show that it's cool to be nice and that bullying is never okay.

Remember, if you see someone else being bullied, you have the power to make a difference. By working together, we can create a world where everyone is treated with respect and kindness.

QUESTIONS FOR YOUR JOURNAL— THINKING ABOUT BULLYING AND SPREADING POSITIVITY

1. Have you ever witnessed bullying happening to someone else? How did it make you feel? What did you do to help?

2. Can you think of a time when you or someone else was kind to someone who needed it? How did it make you feel?

3. What are some ways that you can be a positive influence on those around you? How can you spread kindness and positivity?

4. Have you ever been bullied or teased by someone? How did it make you feel? What did you do about it?
5. What are some things you can do to prevent bullying from happening in the first place?
6. How can you create a safe and welcoming environment for everyone?
7. Write about a time when someone was kind to you. How did it make you feel? Write a letter to someone who is being bullied. What would you say to them?
8. Think of three ways you can spread positivity today. Write them down and make a plan to follow through.

In the next chapter, we'll explore some ways that you can make money, as well as tips for saving and budgeting. Whether you're looking to buy a new toy or save up for something big, these skills will come in handy both now and in the future. So let's dive in and learn how to make the most of your money!

CHAPTER 10
TIPS FOR MAKING AND SAVING MONEY

Have you ever wanted to buy something special, but didn't have enough money? Or maybe just wanted to save for a rainy day? As a kid, you may not have a lot of money to work with, but that doesn't mean you can't start learning how to manage it. In this chapter, you'll learn some great tips and tricks for earning money, as well as how to save and budget your funds wisely. You don't need to have a lot of money to get started–with a little bit of know-how and some dedication, you can make your money work for you!

SAVING VS. SPENDING

One of the biggest things to learn about money is how to save it and spend it wisely. You may have got some money as a gift and didn't know what to do with it. Or maybe you've been trying to save up for something cool but haven't been able to keep your money.

Saving and spending are two different ways to use your money. Saving means putting some of your money aside for later. This is money that you don't spend right away but keep in a safe place like a bank or a piggy bank. Spending, on the other hand, is using your money to buy something right now, like a toy or a snack.

Think of saving and spending like a game. When you save your money, you're playing the long game. You're thinking about what you might want or need in the future, and you're putting money aside to make sure you can afford it. When you spend your money, you're playing the short game. You're thinking about what you want or need right now, and you're using your money to get it.

Both saving and spending can be fun, but they have different results. When you save your money, you're building up your savings so you can afford things that you need in the future. When you spend your money, you're using it up, and you might not have as much left over for other things you want or need later.

What are wants and needs?

Figuring out what to save and spend all starts with knowing the difference between wants and needs. A "want" is something that you wish you had for fun or entertainment— like candy or a video game. A "need" is something that you can't live easily without. When you're deciding whether to save or spend your money, it's important to think about whether it's a want or a need. If it's a need, like school supplies, you'll definitely have to spend some money on it. But if it's a want, you might think about saving up for it instead of spending all your money right away.

But for you, since you probably won't need to pay for the "needs," you will have to think about if it is something you want *now* or something you will want in the future. This is the difference between a bag of candies now and a new game that you will play with for years.

How to stay organized

Another big principle of saving vs. spending is being organized. You can only make good decisions about your money if you know how much you have and how much you're spending. One way to stay organized is to write down everything you make and everything you spend. You can use a note-book, a piece of paper, a computer, or even a phone app if you like. Write down all the money you get, like allowance, gifts, or money you earn from doing chores. Then, write down everything you spend money on, like snacks, toys, or movies. This will help you see where your money is going and how much you have left over.

Once you know how much money you have and what you're spending it on, you can start thinking about saving. Saving is really important because it means you're putting your money aside for something that you value in life. Maybe you want to save up for a new bike or a trip to the movies with your friends. Whatever it is, you'll need to set a goal for yourself and start putting some money aside each week or each month. Even if you can only save a little bit at a time, it will add up over time and you'll be able to reach your goal soon enough.

When you're trying to save money, an essential skill is learning to avoid something called an "impulse buy." An impulse buy is when you see something you really want and buy it right away without really thinking about it. It's okay to treat yourself sometimes, but if you're always buying things on impulse, you'll never be able to save up for the things that really matter to you. So, before you buy something, take a minute to think about whether it's a want or a need, and whether it's really worth spending your money on.

On the other hand, spending can also be necessary because it means you're enjoying the things you have and using them to their fullest. It's okay to spend money on things that make you happy or help you learn new things. For example, if you love playing soccer, it's okay to spend money on a new soccer ball or some new cleats. But again, it's essential to think about whether it's a want or a need, and whether it's really worth spending your money on.

TIPS FOR MAKING MONEY AS A KID

Making money can be really fun, and it's a great way to learn about responsibility and hard work. There are lots of different ways you can make money, and it doesn't have to be complicated!

Here are some ideas to get you started:

Babysitting   Dog   Pet
                   walking   sitting

1. Babysitting: If you're responsible and enjoy being around kids, babysitting can be a great way to make some extra money. Talk to your parents or other adults in your life about finding families who need a babysitter.
2. Yard work: Do you enjoy being outside and getting your hands dirty? Offer to help your neighbors with their yard work, like mowing the lawn or pulling weeds.
3. Pet sitting: If you love animals, pet sitting can be a fun way to make money. Offer to take care of pets while their owners are away on vacation or out of town.
4. Selling crafts: Do you enjoy making things with your hands? You can sell your crafts at local markets or online.
5. Doing odd jobs: Offer to help adults in your community with tasks like organizing their garage, cleaning their house, or running errands for them.
6. Lemonade stand: A classic way to make money during the summer is by running a lemonade stand. Set up a table and make some homemade lemonade to sell to people passing by.
7. Recycling: Collecting and recycling cans and bottles can be a great way to make a little extra money while also helping the environment.
8. Dog walking: Offer to walk your neighbor's dogs for a fee. This is a great way to get exercise while making money.

9. Car washing: Offer to wash and detail cars for people in your community. You can charge a flat fee or ask for donations.

QUESTIONS— FINDING WAYS TO MAKE AND MANAGE MONEY

1. What are some fun activities you enjoy doing in your free time that could potentially make you money?
2. What are some jobs that involve your favorite hobby or activity?
3. What are some ways you can save money while still enjoying your favorite activities?
4. How can you balance spending money on things you love with saving money for the future?
5. What are some creative ways you can save money, while still enjoying the things you love?
6. How can you make a budget that allows you to enjoy your hobbies and save money at the same time?
7. What are some things you could sell to make extra money?
8. How can you use your skills and talents to earn money doing something fun?
9. How can you set financial goals for yourself while still enjoying your hobbies?
10. What are some ways you can use your money to help others or give back to your community?
11. What are some things you can do to make sure you're managing your money wisely?

Remember, when you're trying to make money, it's important to be responsible and dependable. Show up on time, do a good job, and be polite and friendly. And don't forget to have fun! Making money can be a great way to learn new skills and make new friends.

In the next chapter, we'll jump into the life skills of taking care of yourself and your body! You will learn all about health, hygiene, sleep, eating, exercise, and more!

CHAPTER 11
HEALTH AND HYGIENE BASICS

Keeping yourself healthy and clean will make sure you stay feeling great and avoid getting sick. By practicing good hygiene habits, you can keep germs and bacteria away and prevent illnesses from spreading. So, get ready to explore the fascinating world of health and hygiene, and learn some fun and helpful tips for taking care of yourself!

WHAT IS PERSONAL HYGIENE?

Hygiene is a really big part of keeping your body clean and healthy. It means doing things like washing your hands, brushing your teeth, and taking baths or showers. When you practice good hygiene, you can stop germs and bacteria from spreading, which can help you avoid getting sick.

Here are some tips to practice good hygiene (Northwestern Medicine, 2022):

1. Wash your hands often - make sure you use soap and warm water for at least 20 seconds (that's about as long as it takes to sing "Happy Birthday" twice). Wash your hands before you eat, after you use the bathroom, and after you cough or sneeze.

2. Cover your mouth when you cough or sneeze - use a tissue or your elbow to cover your mouth and nose. This will help prevent germs from spreading to other people.

3. Brush your teeth twice a day - brush your teeth in the morning and before you go to bed. Use toothpaste with fluoride to help keep your teeth strong and healthy.

4. Take a bath or shower every day - this will help keep your skin clean and healthy. Make sure you use soap and warm water to wash your body and your hair.

5. Keep your living space clean - help keep your home clean by picking up after yourself and helping with chores like dusting and vacuuming.

6. Use hand sanitizer when you can't wash your hands - sometimes you might not be near a sink, so it's a good idea to carry hand sanitizer with you. Make sure you know how to use it properly.

7. Don't share personal items - things like towels, combs, and utensils can spread germs, so it's best to use your own personal items and not share them with others.

8. Stay home when you're sick - if you're feeling sick, it is best to stay home and rest. This will help prevent germs from spreading to other people, and give your body a chance to recover.

KEEPING YOUR AMAZING BODY HEALTHY

Keeping your body healthy is key to your overall well-being. When you're healthy, you feel better, have more energy, and can do more things. Here's a guide to help you keep your body healthy (Northwestern Medicine, 2022)!

Getting enough sleep

Did you know that getting enough sleep is a really big part of your general health? It's true! Sleep is like food and water for your body— it's something you need to stay healthy and feel your best.

When you sleep, your body and brain get a chance to rest and recharge. This means that when you wake up in the morning, you'll feel refreshed and ready to take on the day! Getting enough sleep also helps you do better in school and sports, and helps you be more alert and focused during the day.

How much sleep do you need? It depends on your age! Here's a general guideline:

- Preschoolers (ages 3-5): 10-13 hours per day
- School-age children (ages 6-12): 9-12 hours per day
- Teens (ages 13-18): 8-10 hours per day

If you're not getting enough sleep, you might feel tired, grumpy, and have a hard time focusing. You might also have trouble with your memory and it might be harder to learn new things. It's also harder to stay healthy when you're not getting enough sleep, because your body needs that time to repair itself and fight off germs and illnesses.

So, how can you make sure you're getting enough sleep? Here are some tips:

- Stick to a regular bedtime and wake-up time, even on weekends.
- Create a relaxing bedtime routine, like taking a bath or reading a book.
- Make sure your bedroom is quiet, dark, and cool.
- Avoid electronics before bedtime, like TV, tablets, or phones, because the light can make it harder to fall asleep.
- Don't eat a big meal right before bed.

Remember, getting enough sleep is just as essential as eating healthy and exercising. So make sure you're giving your body the rest it needs, and you'll be ready to take on the day!

Eating a balanced diet

Eating a balanced diet is one of the most important things you can do to keep your body healthy. This means eating a variety of foods from different food groups, such as (Northwestern Medicine, 2022):

- Fruits and vegetables: these are great sources of vitamins, minerals, and fiber. Try to eat at least five servings of fruits and vegetables every day.
- Grains: these are huge sources of energy, and provide essential nutrients such as fiber and B vitamins. Choose whole grains whenever possible, such as whole wheat bread and brown rice.
- Protein: protein plays a role in building and repairing muscles, and also helps keep you feeling full. Good sources of protein include lean meats, fish, beans, and tofu.
- Dairy: dairy products are great sources of calcium, which helps build strong bones. Choose low-fat or fat-free dairy products, such as milk, yogurt, and cheese.

The importance of moderation

Moderation means not having too much of something, but also not having too little. When it comes to eating, moderation means eating just the right amount of food to keep your body healthy.

Why does moderation even matter? Well, if you eat too much of one thing, it can be bad for your health. For example, if you eat too much candy or chips, it can make you feel sick, and too much sugar can be bad for your teeth. On the other hand, if you don't eat enough of certain foods, your body might not get all the nutrients it needs to stay healthy and strong.

That's why it's important to eat a variety of different foods in moderation. You can enjoy your favorite treats once in a while, but it's also essential to eat plenty of fruits and vegetables, whole grains, lean protein, and healthy fats. This way, you can get all the nutrients your body needs to grow and be healthy, while still enjoying the foods you love.

Here are a few tips for you to learn to eat a balanced diet (Northwestern Medicine, 2022):

- Make half your plate fruits and vegetables. Try to eat a variety of different colors to get different nutrients. Fruits and vegetables are crucial for your body because they contain many vitamins and minerals that help your body function properly. They are also low in calories and high in fiber, which can help you feel full and satisfied. When you eat a variety of different colors of fruits and vegetables, you can get a wide range of nutrients. For example, red fruits and vegetables like tomatoes and strawberries contain lycopene, which is good for your heart, while green leafy vegetables like spinach and kale contain iron and calcium, which are needed to keep your bones healthy.
- Limit Sugary and Fatty Foods: Sugary and fatty foods can be high in calories and low in nutrients. Eating too many of these foods can lead to weight gain, which can increase your risk of health problems like diabetes and heart disease. It's okay to have these foods once in a while as a treat, but try to limit your intake and choose healthier options instead.
- Choosing lean sources of protein: Protein is important for building and repairing your body's tissues. However, not all protein sources are created equal. Some sources of protein, like red meat, can be high in unhealthy fat, which can raise your cholesterol and increase your risk of heart disease. Choosing lean sources of protein, like chicken, fish, and beans, can help you get the protein your body needs without the added unhealthy fat.
- Drink plenty of water throughout the day. Water is essential for your body because it helps transport nutrients, regulate body temperature, and remove waste. Drinking enough water can also help you feel full, which can prevent overeating. It's important to drink water throughout the day, even when you're not thirsty, to stay properly hydrated. Sugary drinks like soda and juice can be high in calories and sugar, which can lead to weight gain and other health problems. Try to limit your intake of these drinks and choose water instead.

- Eating enough whole grains: Whole grains are a good source of carbohydrates, which provide energy for your body. However, not all grains are created equal. Refined grains like white bread and white rice have had the healthy parts removed, leaving behind mostly empty calories (which don't make you feel full). Whole grains like brown rice, whole wheat bread, and quinoa are better choices because they contain fiber, which helps keep you full and can lower your risk of heart disease and other health problems.

IDEAS TO GET MOVING!

Exercise is another massive part of keeping your body healthy. Regular physical activity can help improve your mood, reduce stress, and help keep your body in shape. When you exercise, you're not only keeping your muscles and bones strong, but you're also keeping your heart healthy and your mind sharp. Here are some tips for staying active (Northwestern Medicine, 2022):

- Aim for at least 60 minutes of physical activity every day. This can include activities like walking, biking, dancing, or playing sports.
- Find activities that you enjoy, so you'll be more likely to stick with them. For example, if you like dancing, try taking a dance class.

- Make exercise a part of your daily routine. For example, you could walk or bike to school instead of taking the bus or car.
- Take active breaks throughout the day, especially if you're sitting for long periods of time. Try doing jumping jacks or stretching.
- Exercise with friends or family members, so you can motivate each other and have fun together.

Here are a few exercise ideas that can make movement fun (Northwestern Medicine, 2022):

Jump rope— Grab a jump rope and see how many jumps you can do in a row. Jumping rope is a great way to get your heart pumping and improve your coordination. You can do it alone or with friends and challenge each other to see who can jump the most times in a row.

Dancing— Put on your favorite music and dance around the house. Dancing is a fun way to get moving and improve your flexibility and balance. You can make up your own dance moves or follow along with a video tutorial.

Yoga— Try some simple yoga poses to stretch your body and improve your flexibility. Yoga can help you feel more calm and centered while also improving your strength and balance. You can find lots of beginner yoga videos online to get started.

Hiking— Take a walk on a nature trail and enjoy the fresh air. Hiking is a great way to explore nature while also getting some exercise. You can hike on a nearby trail or visit a national park to see some beautiful scenery.

Soccer— Play a game of soccer with your friends or family. Soccer is a fun sport that involves running, kicking, and teamwork. You can play on a soccer field or in a park and practice your skills with drills and games.

Swimming— Go for a swim and have fun in the pool. Swimming is a great way to cool off in the summer while also getting some exercise. You can swim laps or play games in the pool with friends and family.

Bike riding— Ride your bike around the neighborhood or on a bike path. Biking is a fun way to explore your neighborhood and get some exercise. You can ride alone or with friends and family and practice your skills on different terrain.

Trampoline— Jump on a trampoline and have fun bouncing around. Trampolining can be a fun and challenging way to improve your balance and coordination. You can jump alone or with friends and family and try different tricks and flips.

Gymnastics— Try some simple gymnastics moves like cartwheels and handstands. Gymnastics can help you improve your strength, flexibility, and coordination. You can practice at a gymnastics gym or at home with a mat.

Basketball— Shoot some hoops with your friends or family. Basketball is a fun sport that involves running, jumping, and teamwork. You can practice your shooting and dribbling skills and play games with friends and family.

Skating— Roller skating or ice skating can be a fun way to get moving. Skating can help improve your balance and coordination while also getting your heart pumping. You can skate at a rink or on a local trail.

Tennis— Play a game of tennis with a friend or family member. Tennis is a fun sport that involves running, hitting, and teamwork. You can practice your skills with drills and games and play on a tennis court or in a park.

Frisbee— Throw a frisbee back and forth with a friend or family member. Frisbee is a fun and easy activity that can be done anywhere. You can practice your throwing and catching skills and play games with friends and family.

Jumping jacks— Do a set of jumping jacks to get your heart rate up. Jumping jacks are a simple and effective exercise that can be done anywhere. You can do them alone or with friends and family and see how many you can do in a row.

Walking— Take a walk around the block or with your family to explore the neighborhood. Walking is a simple and easy way to get moving and explore your surroundings. You can walk alone or with friends and family.

Now you know all about how to keep your body healthy! You've learned about the importance of eating a balanced diet, getting enough exercise, practicing good hygiene, and getting enough sleep. By making these healthy choices, you're giving your body the fuel it needs to feel its best.

But did you know that you can also play a big role in cooking healthy meals at home? In the next chapter, you'll learn all about how you can help out in the kitchen and even start cooking on your own! Cooking is a fun and rewarding way to take control of your health and make sure you're eating meals that make your body feel good.

So get ready to put on your chef's hat and apron, and let's get cooking!

CHAPTER 12
FOOD AND COOKING SKILLS

Cooking is a super fun and creative way to make delicious meals for yourself and your family. From learning how to boil an egg to preparing a complete meal, the ability to cook and handle food can help you be more independent and responsible.

In this chapter, you'll learn how to get involved with cooking, starting with simple tasks like setting the table and gradually working your way up to preparing a full meal all on your own. So, throw on your apron, grab your utensils, and let's get cooking together!

BASIC COOKING AND KITCHEN SKILLS YOU CAN LEARN TODAY!

Are you ready to learn some awesome basic cooking skills? Here are some tips to get you started (Heart and Stroke, 2023):

1. Setting the table: To set the table, you'll need a plate, a fork, a knife, a spoon, and a glass. Make sure to place everything in the right spot! The plate goes in the center, the fork goes on the left and the spoon and knife go on the right, and the glass goes above the knife. Then you can add a napkin either to the left of the fork or on top of the dinner plate.

2. Keeping things clean: Always wash your hands before handling any food. It's important to keep your kitchen surfaces and utensils clean to avoid spreading germs. Use soap and warm water to wash your hands for at least 20 seconds, and wipe down surfaces with a clean cloth or paper towel.

3. Understanding basic measuring: Measuring ingredients like flour, sugar, and milk is important in cooking. Use measuring cups and spoons to make sure you add the right amount of each ingredient. For liquids, use a liquid measuring cup and make sure to read the measurements at eye level.

4. Using a peeler and grater: A peeler is used to remove the skin from fruits and vegetables. Hold the peeler in one hand and the fruit or vegetable in the other, and gently scrape away the skin. A grater is used to shred things like cheese or carrots. Hold the grater with one hand and the food with the other, and grate back and forth.

Pictured above, someone using a grater.

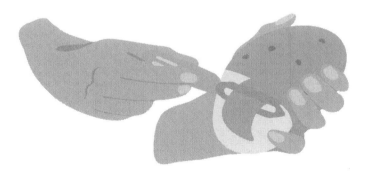

Pictured above, someone using a peeler.

5. Tips for following simple recipes: Read the recipe carefully before starting to make sure you have all the ingredients and equipment you need. Follow the steps in order, and don't skip any! If you're not sure what a word means, ask an adult or look it up.

6. Preparing a balanced lunch: A balanced lunch should include protein, veggies, and healthy fats. For example, you could make a turkey and cheese sandwich on whole grain bread, with carrot sticks and hummus on the side. Or, you could make a salad with chicken, spinach, and avocado.

7. Baking skills: Baking is a fun way to get creative in the kitchen! When baking, it's important to measure ingredients accurately and follow the recipe carefully. Use an oven mitt when taking things out of the oven, and let things cool before eating.

8. Using the stove: Using the stove can be intimidating, but with an adult's help, you can learn to cook simple things like scrambled eggs or pasta. Always use pot holders or oven mitts when handling hot pots and pans.

9. Handling raw meat carefully: Raw meat can carry harmful bacteria, so it's important to handle it carefully. Always wash your hands after touching raw meat, and use separate cutting boards and utensils for meat and other foods.

10. How to boil an egg: Boiling an egg is a great basic cooking skill to have. Start by placing an egg in boiling water for about 10 minutes, then cool it down and peel it carefully. You can eat boiled eggs on their own or use them in recipes like egg salad.

11. Cleaning up after cooking: Cleaning up after cooking is just as important as the cooking itself. Make sure to wash your dishes, clean your surfaces, and put away any ingredients you used. This will help keep your kitchen clean and tidy!

Let's move on to talk about some cooking terms that you are going to need to know if you want to get started on your journey in the kitchen.

UNDERSTANDING COOKING WORDS

Here's a list of cooking words and terms that every kid should know, along with some explanations to help you understand them better (Heart and Stroke, 2023):

- Preheat: This means to turn on the oven to the temperature specified in the recipe, before you start cooking.

- Sauté: This means cooking something quickly in a hot pan with a little bit of oil, stirring it often so that it doesn't burn.
- Simmer: This means to cook something liquid on low heat, so that it bubbles gently but doesn't boil over.
- Boil: This means cooking something in water that is bubbling rapidly.
- Chop: This means cutting something into small pieces using a knife.
- Mince: This means to cut something into very small pieces using a knife or a food processor.
- Dice: This means cutting something into small, even cubes.
- Grate: This means shredding something into small pieces using a grater.
- Whisk: This means to mix ingredients together quickly and vigorously using a whisk or a fork.
- Stir: This means mixing ingredients together gently using a spoon.
- Fold: This means to mix ingredients together gently, using a spatula, so that the mixture stays light and airy.
- Knead: This means to work the dough with your hands, folding it over and pressing it down, to make it smooth and elastic.
- Bake: This means to cook something in the oven, usually at a specific temperature and for a specific amount of time.
- Roast: This means to cook something in the oven, usually at a high temperature, to give it a crispy outside and a tender inside.
- Grill: This means to cook something over an open flame, either outdoors or on a grill pan, to give it a smoky flavor.
- Marinate: This means soaking something in a mixture of ingredients, like oil, vinegar, and spices, to add flavor and tenderness.

SIMPLE RECIPES TO TRY OUT

Here are a few simple recipes for you to try out! Along with detailed instructions to help you along the way:

Grilled Cheese Sandwich

- Spread butter on one side of each slice of bread.
- Put a slice of cheese between the two slices of bread, with the buttered sides facing out.
- Heat a pan over medium heat and put the sandwich in the pan.
- Cook for 2-3 minutes on each side, until the cheese is melted and the bread is golden brown.

Fruit Salad

- Cut up your favorite fruits, like apples, bananas, strawberries, and grapes, into small pieces.
- Put the fruit in a bowl and mix it together.
- You can add a little bit of honey or lemon juice for extra flavor, if you like.

Macaroni and Cheese

- Cook 8 oz of macaroni according to the package instructions.
- Drain the macaroni and put it back in the pot.
- Add 1 cup of shredded cheese and 1/4 cup of milk to the pot.
- Cook on low heat until the cheese is melted and the macaroni is coated in cheese.

Pancakes (All Recipes)

- In a bowl, mix together 1 1/2 cups of all-purpose flour, 3 tablespoons of granulated sugar, 1 tablespoon of baking powder, and 1/2 teaspoon of salt.
- Add 1 1/4 cups of milk, 2 large eggs, and 1/4 cup of melted butter to the bowl, and mix everything together until the batter is smooth.
- Heat a pan over medium heat and add a little bit of oil or butter to the pan.
- Use a ladle to pour the batter into the pan, making pancakes that are about 4 inches in diameter.
- Cook for 2-3 minutes on each side, until the pancakes are golden brown.

Smoothie

- Blend together your favorite fruits and a little bit of yogurt or milk until smooth.
- You can add a handful of spinach or kale for extra nutrients, if you like.
- Pour the smoothie into a glass and enjoy!

Quesadilla

- Add a little olive oil to a pan
- Put a tortilla in the pan over medium heat.
- Sprinkle shredded cheese and any other toppings you like, such as cooked chicken or veggies, on one half of the tortilla.
- Fold the other half of the tortilla over the toppings and press down with a spatula.
- Cook for 2-3 minutes on each side, until the cheese is melted and the tortilla is golden brown.

Trail Mix

- Mix together your favorite nuts, like almonds or cashews, with dried fruit, like raisins or cranberries.
- You can also add in some chocolate chips or pretzels for a sweet and salty treat.

Baked Chicken Tenders

- Cut chicken breasts into strips.
- Dip the chicken strips into a beaten egg, then coat them in breadcrumbs mixed with some salt and pepper.
- Place the chicken strips on a baking sheet lined with parchment paper.
- Bake in the oven at 400°F for 15-20 minutes, until the chicken is cooked through and the breadcrumbs are golden brown.

Egg Scramble

- Crack 2-3 eggs into a bowl and whisk them together.
- Add salt, pepper, and any other toppings you like, such as shredded cheese, chopped veggies, or cooked ham.
- Heat a pan over medium heat and add a little bit of butter or oil to the pan.
- Pour the egg mixture into the pan and cook for 2-3 minutes on each side, until the eggs are set and the cheese is melted.

Banana Bread

- Preheat your oven to 350°F (175°C) and grease a 9x5 inch loaf pan.
- In a mixing bowl, mash 2-3 ripe bananas until smooth.
- Add 1 1/2 cups all-purpose flour, 1/3 cup granulated sugar, 1 teaspoon baking powder, 1/2 teaspoon salt, and 1 beaten egg to the bowl. Mix everything together until the batter is smooth.
- Pour the batter into the greased loaf pan.
- Bake the banana bread in the preheated oven for 45-50 minutes, or until the bread is golden brown and a toothpick inserted into the center comes out clean.
- Remove the pan from the oven and let it cool for 10 minutes before removing the bread from the pan. Cool on a wire rack before slicing and serving.

Baked Apples

- Cut an apple into thin slices and put the slices in a baking dish.
- Sprinkle cinnamon and a little bit of sugar over the apples.
- Bake in the oven at 350°F for 15-20 minutes, until the apples are soft and the cinnamon is fragrant.

Enjoy trying out these new recipes, and remember to always have fun and be safe in the kitchen! In the next chapter, we will keep talking about household tasks, but now on the topic of chores. They aren't always fun... but did you know that they can be beneficial for you?

CHAPTER 13
LET'S TALK ABOUT CHORES

Now we're going to talk about something that may not seem like much fun, but is actually really important for your future: chores!

Chores are tasks or responsibilities that you are expected to complete at home, such as cleaning your room, doing the dishes, or helping with laundry. While they may seem like a hassle, chores are actually really important for a few key reasons.

Firstly, chores teach you important life skills that you will need as you get older. When you become a teenager and eventually an adult, you will need to know how to take care of yourself and your home. By doing chores now, you are practicing these skills and building the foundation for responsibility and independence.

Secondly, chores help you prepare for the responsibilities of being a teenager. As you get older, you will have more responsibilities, such as schoolwork, extracurricular activities, and maybe even a part-time job. By doing chores now, you are learning how to manage your time and balance your responsibilities. This will help you to be more prepared and successful as you navigate your teenage years.

Finally, chores help you gain independence and responsibility. When you complete chores on your own, you are showing your parents or guardians that you can be trusted with important tasks. This can lead to more independence and freedom, as well as increased trust from the adults in your life. It also helps you to feel more confident and capable, which is an important part of growing up.

Let's dive right in to some ways you can take on more responsibility around the house and keep your tasks organized!

KEEPING YOUR RESPONSIBILITIES ORGANIZED

Do you ever feel like you have so many chores and tasks to do that it's hard to keep them all organized? Don't worry; you're not alone! But the good news is that there are some simple things you can do to keep everything in order and make sure you get everything done.

One way to keep your chores and tasks organized is to make a list. You can either use a piece of paper and a pen, or you can use an app on your phone or tablet. Write down everything you need to do, and then check each item

95

off as you complete it. This will help you stay on track and make sure you don't forget anything important.

Another way to stay organized is to set a schedule. Decide when you're going to do each chore or task, and then stick to that schedule. This will help you manage your time more effectively and make sure you have enough time to do everything you need to do.

If you have siblings, trading off chores can also be really helpful. This means that one day you do the dishes, and the next day your sibling does them. This way, you both get a break and you can focus on other tasks that need to be done.

Remember, staying organized and keeping track of your chores and tasks is an important part of being responsible and independent. It can also help you manage your time more effectively and reduce stress.

BASIC CHORES AND HOUSEHOLD SKILLS

Are you ready to become a chore pro? Here's a guide to some basic chores you can master (Eisenberg, 2016):

- Basic Laundry Skills— Laundry is an important chore to learn, and it's not as hard as you might think! First, separate your clothes into piles - whites, colors, and darks. Then, put each pile into the washing machine with the right amount of detergent. After the cycle is done, move the clothes to the dryer and add a dryer sheet. Don't forget to fold and put away your clothes when they're dry!

- Basic Dish Washing— Dish washing is another important chore. Start by rinsing off any leftover food from the dishes. Then, add dish soap and hot water to the sink and wash each dish one by one. Rinse off any remaining soap and place the dishes in the dish rack to dry. Don't forget to put away the clean dishes when they're dry!
- Mowing the Lawn— If you have a lawn, mowing it can be a great way to get outside and get some exercise. First, make sure you ask a parent to help you out and teach you a few times before you do it on your own. You will also need to know how to safely operate the mower and wear protective gear like closed-toe shoes and eye protection. Then, mow the lawn in rows, making sure to overlap each pass to get an even cut.
- Sweeping and Vacuuming— Keeping your floors clean is important too! Grab a broom and dustpan to sweep up any debris or dirt. For carpets, use a vacuum to suck up any dirt or dust. Make sure to clean under furniture and in corners too!

- Recycling— Recycling is important for taking care of our planet. Make sure you know what can and can't be recycled in your area. Rinse out any containers and separate them into the right bins. Don't forget to break down any cardboard boxes to save space!
- Washing Windows— Keeping your windows clean can make a big difference in how your home looks. First, gather supplies like a squeegee, bucket, and window cleaner. Then, spray the cleaner onto the window and use the squeegee to wipe away any dirt and liquid. Finish by wiping the edges with a clean cloth.
- Dusting Furniture— Dusting furniture is important to keep your home clean and healthy. Use a microfiber cloth to wipe down surfaces, making sure to get into any nooks and crannies. You can also use a feather duster to reach high places or delicate items.
- Washing the Car— Washing a car may seem easy, but it requires attention to detail and hard work. Start by hosing off any loose dirt and debris. Then, use a sponge and bucket of soapy water to wash the car, making sure to get all the nooks and crannies. Rinse off the soap and dry the car with a clean towel to finish.
- Organizing a Closet— Organizing a closet can be a big project, but it's a great way to practice decision-making and time management skills. Start by emptying out the entire closet and sorting items into categories like "keep," "donate," and "throw away." Then, use storage containers or hanging organizers to put everything back in an organized way.
- Cleaning the Bathroom— Cleaning the bathroom may not be the most fun chore, but it's an important one. Start by wiping down the sink, counter, and toilet with a disinfectant cleaner. Scrub the shower and bathtub with a cleaner designed for those surfaces. Finally, sweep and mop the floor to finish the job.

You're a pro now! Just remember that these skills will take time and practice. However, simply showing your parents that you care and are responsible enough to do things on your own will help you gain independence. In the next chapter, you'll discover some skills that can help keep you safe and healthy… First Aid skills!

CHAPTER 14
FIRST AID SKILLS

It's important to know how to help someone who is hurt or injured, and it's even more important to stay calm and focused when you're trying to help. In this chapter, you'll learn about some basic first aid skills that you can use to help someone in need. We'll talk about how to assess the situation, how to call for help if you need it, and how to perform some basic first aid techniques like treating cuts and bruises and helping someone who is choking or having trouble breathing.

Remember, it's always better to be prepared and know what to do in case of an emergency. So read on, and learn some ways you can become a more helpful and responsible member of your community!

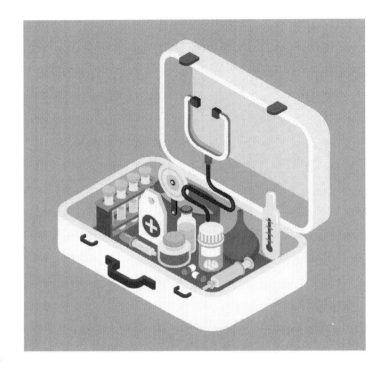

HOW TO MAKE A FIRST AID KIT

Having a first aid kit ready can be very helpful when you or someone you know gets hurt. Here's a guide on how to make your own first aid kit:

Materials you'll need:

- A container or box to hold your first aid supplies
- Band-Aids in different sizes
- Gauze pads
- Adhesive tape
- Antiseptic wipes or cream
- Disposable gloves
- Scissors
- Tweezers
- A thermometer

Here are the instructions to create your first aid kit (Jacobs, 2014):

1. Choose a container or box to hold your first aid supplies. It could be a plastic container with a lid, a small toolbox, or a pencil case. Make sure it's big enough to fit all the supplies.
2. Gather the supplies you need. You can find them at a drugstore or grocery store.
3. Put the Band-Aids, gauze pads, adhesive tape, and antiseptic wipes or cream in your container.
4. Add disposable gloves, scissors, and tweezers to your kit. You can use scissors to cut gauze and tape and tweezers to remove splinters.
5. Don't forget to include a thermometer in your kit. This will help you check if someone has a fever.
6. Once you have all your supplies in the container, close the lid and make sure everything is secure.
7. Keep your first aid kit in a safe and accessible place, like a closet or a drawer in your bedroom.

Remember to always ask an adult for help if you're not sure what to do. Stay safe and be prepared to help others in case of an emergency!

FIRST AID SKILLS YOU NEED TO KNOW

It's always important to know basic first aid to keep yourself and others safe. Here's a guide on first aid basics (Jacobs, 2014):

Nosebleeds

Nosebleeds happen when blood comes out of your nose. They can be scary, but they usually aren't serious. Nosebleeds can happen for a few different reasons, like dry air, picking your nose, or getting hit in the nose.

If you get a nosebleed, here are some things you can do to help:

1. Sit down and lean forward slightly: This can help keep the blood from going down your throat.
2. Pinch your nostrils together: Use your fingers to pinch your nostrils together right below the bony part of your nose. Keep them pinched for about 10 minutes. This can help stop the bleeding.
3. Breathe through your mouth: While you're pinching your nostrils, breathe through your mouth.
4. Don't blow your nose: Blowing your nose can make the bleeding worse. Try to avoid blowing your nose for a few hours after the nosebleed.
5. Tell an adult: If the bleeding doesn't stop after 10-15 minutes, you should tell an adult and go see a doctor.

Burns

Burns are injuries to the skin that happen when something hot, like fire, steam, or a hot stove, touches your skin. Burns can range from mild, like a sunburn, to severe, like a third-degree burn. Burns can be very painful and can cause blisters, swelling, and redness.

If you get a burn, here are some things you can do to help:

1. Cool the burn: Run cool (not cold) water over the burn for at least 10 minutes. This can help reduce pain and swelling.
2. Remove any tight clothing or jewelry: If you have a burn on your arm or leg, for example, remove any clothing or jewelry that's tight or might make the burn worse.
3. Apply an ointment: Put a thin layer of aloe vera gel or antibiotic ointment, like Neosporin, on the burn. This can help promote healing and prevent infection.
4. Cover the burn: Put a clean, dry bandage or gauze over the burn to keep it clean and protected. Change the bandage every day or if it gets wet or dirty.

Small cuts and scratches

Cuts and scratches are injuries to the skin that happen when something sharp or rough touches your skin. A cut is when the skin is broken and bleeding, while a scratch is when the skin is scraped but not broken. Cuts and scratches can happen anywhere on your body, like your arms, legs, or face.

If you get a cut or a scratch, here are some things you can do to help:

1. Clean the cut or scratch: Use soap and warm water to clean the injured area. Gently pat it dry with a clean towel.
2. Stop the bleeding: If the cut is bleeding, hold a clean cloth or bandage over it and apply pressure for a few minutes until the bleeding stops.
3. Apply an ointment: Put a thin layer of antibiotic ointment, like Neosporin, on the cut or scratch. This can help prevent infection and

promote healing.

4. Cover the cut or scratch: Put a clean bandage or gauze over the cut or scratch to keep it clean and protected. Change the bandage every day or if it gets wet or dirty.

Remember, if the cut or scratch is really deep or if it doesn't stop bleeding after a few minutes, you should tell an adult and go see a doctor. They can help you figure out if there's something more serious going on and give you the right treatment.

Swelling

Swelling is when a part of your body gets bigger than usual, like when you get a bump or a bruise. It can also happen when you hurt a joint, like your ankle or your wrist. Swelling happens because your body is trying to protect the injured area by sending extra blood and fluid to the area.

If you have swelling, there are a few things you can do to help:

1. Rest the injured area: Try not to use the injured area as much as possible. If it's your ankle or your knee, try to stay off your feet or use crutches to help you walk.
2. Ice the injured area: Put an ice pack or a bag of frozen vegetables wrapped in a towel on the injured area. Leave it on for 10-20 minutes at a time, a few times a day. This can help reduce swelling and pain.
3. Elevate the injured area: If possible, elevate the injured area above your heart. This can help reduce swelling and improve blood flow.

Choking

Choking is a scary situation, but it's important to know what to do if someone is choking. Here's a guide on how to react to choking:

1. Stay calm and assess the situation. If someone is choking, they may be coughing, wheezing, or gasping for air. If they can't breathe, they may be turning blue or not making any noise at all.
2. If the person can still breathe, encourage them to keep coughing to try and dislodge the object that's stuck in their throat.

3. If the person can't breathe, call for help immediately! Shout for an adult or call 911. Don't waste time trying to help the person by yourself.
4. While waiting for help to arrive, try the Heimlich maneuver. Stand behind the person and wrap your arms around their waist. Make a fist with one hand and place it just above the belly button, then grab your fist with your other hand. Push in and up with a quick thrust. Repeat until the object is dislodged or help arrives.

Remember, choking can be very serious. Stay calm, call for help, and try the Heimlich maneuver if the person can't breathe. You can be a lifesaver if you know what to do in an emergency!

Bruises

Bruises can happen when you bump or hit something hard, and they can be sore and uncomfortable. Here's a guide on how to react to bruises:

1. If you get a bruise, don't panic. It's a common injury and it will usually go away on its own in a few days.
2. If the bruise is painful, you can put an ice pack on it for 10-20 minutes at a time. Wrap the ice pack in a towel to protect your skin from the cold.
3. If the bruise is on your arm or leg, elevate it by propping it up on a pillow or cushion. This can help reduce swelling.
4. You can also take over-the-counter pain relievers like acetaminophen or ibuprofen to help with the pain. Remember to always ask an adult before taking any medication.
5. If the bruise is very large or doesn't go away after a few days, you should see a doctor.
6. If you see someone with a bruise, be gentle and kind. Don't touch the bruise or poke it, as this can be painful.

Remember, bruises are a normal part of life and usually don't require any special treatment.

Concussions

A concussion is a type of brain injury that can happen when you hit your head really hard, like in a sports game or if you accidentally fall and hit your head. When you get a concussion, your brain gets jostled around inside your skull and can cause problems like headaches, dizziness, nausea, confusion, and memory loss.

If you think you or someone else has a concussion, it's important to tell an adult right away. Here are some things you can do:

1. Take a break: If you're playing a sport or doing an activity when you get a concussion, stop right away and take a break. Rest is important to help your brain heal.
2. Tell an adult: Tell an adult what happened and how you're feeling. They can help you figure out what to do next and make sure you get the right medical care.
3. Rest your brain: Avoid activities that could make your symptoms worse, like playing video games or watching TV. Take naps or rest as needed.
4. Follow medical advice: If a doctor or nurse tells you to do something specific, like take medicine or rest for a certain amount of time, make sure you follow their advice.

Remember, if you or someone else is hurt, always reach out to an adult for help. They will be able to provide additional assistance and ensure that you receive the appropriate medical care. Stay safe!

How to Respond in an Emergency

Sometimes emergencies happen, like someone falls down and gets hurt, or there's a fire or an accident. It's important to know what to do in an emergency so you can stay safe and help others.

Here are some things you can do if you're in an emergency situation:

1. Stay calm: Even though emergencies can be scary, it's important to try to stay calm so you can think clearly and make good decisions.
2. Call for help: If you have a phone, call 911 (or your local emergency number) right away. Tell the operator what's happening and where you are. If you don't have a phone, find an adult who can call for help.
3. Stay safe: If there's a fire or other danger, try to get to a safe place. If someone is hurt, try to help them without putting yourself in danger.
4. Talk to emergency responders: When the police, firefighters, or paramedics arrive, it's important to talk to them and answer their questions. They are there to help you, and they need to know what's going on so they can do their job.

Here are some tips for talking to emergency responders:

- Speak clearly: Make sure you speak clearly so the emergency responders can understand you.
- Be honest: Tell the truth about what happened and what you know.
- Stay calm: Even though you might be scared or upset, try to stay calm and answer the questions as best you can.

Remember, in an emergency, it's important to always tell an adult if you or someone else is hurt. Try to stay calm and call for help right away. And when emergency responders arrive, talk to them and help them understand what's going on so they can help you.

In the next chapter you will discover how you can solve problems all on your own! This is an awesome skill that will help you thrive through the rest of your childhood, teenage years, and into adulthood!

CHAPTER 15
LEARNING TO SOLVE PROBLEMS

Do you ever face tough challenges in or out of the classroom? Maybe you struggle with tricky math problems or feel unsure in difficult social situations. Well, guess what? Learning how to problem-solve can help you overcome these challenges and succeed in life!

Problem-solving is a super important skill that helps you think deeply, get creative, and be resourceful. With these skills, you can tackle problems step by step, find great solutions, and stay calm and cool under pressure. These skills are not only helpful now, but they'll be super useful in the future too.

In this chapter, we'll explore lots of different problem-solving strategies that can help you with all kinds of problems. Whether they're simple or super tricky, we'll help you develop the skills you need to solve them. So let's get started and become an awesome problem-solver!

WHAT ARE DECISION-MAKING SKILLS?

As a kid, you make decisions every day, whether it's choosing what to wear or what to have for breakfast. But as you grow older, the decisions you make become more important and can have a bigger impact on your life. That's why it's important to develop good decision-making skills. In this section, we'll explore what decision-making skills are and how to practice them.

Decision-making skills are the ability to choose the best course of action from among several options. They involve analyzing information, weighing the pros and cons, and making a choice based on what you think is best. Good decision-making skills can help you make choices that lead to positive outcomes and avoid choices that can have negative consequences.

Why are Decision-Making Skills Important?

Good decision-making skills are important for several reasons. First, they help you solve problems and make choices that lead to good results. Second,

LIFE SKILLS FOR KIDS

they help you avoid making choices that can have bad results. Third, they help you become more independent and self-sufficient, as you learn to make decisions on your own (Mattingly, 2020).

Let's talk about how you can make tough decisions! Here are some steps you can take (Mattingly, 2020):

- Figure out what decision you need to make: The first step in making a decision is to identify what you need to decide. This could be something like which activity to do after school or what gift to buy for your friend's birthday.
- Next, Make a pros and cons list: One helpful way to make a decision is to create a pros and cons list. This means making two lists - one with all the reasons why you should do something, and another with all the reasons why you shouldn't. Be sure to think about both short-term and long-term consequences.
- After you've made your pros and cons list, take some time to evaluate it. Think about which reasons are the most important to you and which ones have the biggest impact.
- Make a decision: Based on your evaluation, it's time to make a decision. Choose the option that you think is best and will lead to the most positive outcome.
- Think back on your decision: After you've made a decision, take some time to think about it. Think about what you learned from the process and whether or not you're happy with the decision you made. If you're not, think about why and how you could make a different decision in the future.

Decision-making skills can help you solve problems because they teach you how to evaluate different options and choose the best one based on the information you have.

When you're faced with a problem, it can be overwhelming and confusing. But by using similar steps you would use to make a decision, you can break the problem down into smaller parts and figure out what to do next.

WHAT SKILLS DO YOU NEED TO SOLVE A PROBLEM?

Have you ever faced a problem that seemed too hard to solve? Well, guess what? You've got what it takes to become an awesome problem-solver! Let's check out some of the skills you will need in order to tackle any problem (Mattingly, 2020).

- First, you need analysis skills. That means you need to look at the problem closely and figure out what's going on. Try to break the problem down into smaller parts to make it easier to understand.
- Next, you need research skills. That means you should do some investigating to gather information that can help you solve the problem. Try looking online, talking to people, or checking out books at the library.
- Then, you need decision-making skills. That means you need to make choices about what to do next. Think about your options and choose the best one.
- You also need planning skills. That means you should make a plan to solve the problem. Think about what steps you need to take and make a list of them.
- Leadership is also important. That means you should be able to take charge and lead others to help you solve the problem. Try to be a positive role model and encourage others to help out too.
- Organization is key too. That means you should keep track of all the information you gathered and the steps you need to take. Try to keep everything in order and easy to understand.
- Judgment is crucial too. That means you need to make good choices and think about what's best for everyone involved.
- Patience is also super important. That means you should take your time and not rush things. Remember, some problems take time to solve.
- Communication skills are also necessary. That means you should be able to talk to others and explain your ideas clearly. Try to listen to others too and work together to find a solution.

- Lastly, you need initiative. That means you should be brave and take the first steps toward solving the problem. Don't be afraid to try new things and take risks.

STEPS TO SOLVING A PROBLEM

Now that you know the skills you need in order to be a great problem-solver, it's time to learn the *exact* process of how you can solve a problem! Let's jump right in (Mattingly, 2020):

1. Identify the problem: The first step in solving a problem is figuring out what the problem actually is! This might sound obvious, but it's important to take the time to really understand what's going on. For example, if you're having trouble with a math problem, you'll want to make sure you understand what the question is asking before you try to solve it.

2. Gather information: Once you know what the problem is, it's time to gather as much information as possible. This might mean doing research,

asking for help, or even just taking a closer look at the problem itself. Let's say you're trying to fix a broken game or bike. You might need to take it apart to see how it works or look up instructions online to see if there are any common issues.

3. Analyze the problem: Once you have all the information you need, it's time to start breaking down the problem into smaller parts. This can help you understand the problem better and come up with potential solutions. For example, if you're trying to bake a cake and it keeps coming out too dry, you might need to look at different aspects of the recipe (like the amount of liquid or the baking time) to figure out what's going wrong.

4. Think of possible solutions: Now that you have a better understanding of the problem, it's time to start brainstorming solutions. This is where you get to be creative and come up with lots of different ideas! Maybe you can fix the broken toy with some glue or tape, or try a different recipe for the cake.

5. Consider the solutions: Once you have a list of potential solutions, it's time to start thinking about which ones could actually work. Consider things like how much time or money each solution would require, and whether or not it would really solve the problem. For example, if you're trying to clean up a messy room, you might realize that hiring a professional organizer is too expensive, but that breaking the task down into smaller steps (like cleaning one corner at a time) is more manageable.

6. Choose a solution: After you've evaluated all the potential solutions, it's time to pick the one you want to try! This can be tough, but trust your instincts and go with the one that seems most promising.

7. Create a plan: Once you've chosen a solution, it's time to make a plan to put it into action. This might involve writing out specific steps to follow or gathering any materials or resources you'll need. For example, if you're trying to build a birdhouse, you might need to gather wood, nails, and a hammer before you start.

8. Take action: Now that you have a plan, it's time to start taking action! Follow the steps you've laid out, and don't be afraid to ask for help if you need it. Remember, it's okay if things don't go perfectly the first time around - that's part of the problem-solving process.

9. Do a check-in on your progress: As you work on your solution, it's important to keep track of how things are going. Are you making progress? Are there any roadblocks or obstacles that you didn't anticipate? Being aware of these things can help you make adjustments as you go along.

10. Look at the results: Once you've finished implementing your solution, it's time to step back and evaluate the results. Did your solution work? Did you

solve the problem? If not, don't worry - there's always room for improvement. Take what you learned from this experience and apply it to future problem-solving challenges!

Learning how to solve problems isn't just about figuring out what to do; you will need to practice these skills. In the next section, you will discover a list of some awesome activities to help you practice making decisions and solving problems.

ACTIVITIES— PRACTICING MAKING DECISIONS AND SOLVING PROBLEMS

- Board games: Play board games with your friends or family. Games like Monopoly and Scrabble require you to make decisions and solve problems as you play. For instance, in Monopoly, you need to decide which properties to buy and how much to pay for them.
- Treasure hunt: Set up a treasure hunt with clues that require you to solve puzzles and make decisions to find the treasure. For example, you might need to decide which direction to go based on a riddle or a map.
- Escape rooms: Visit an escape room where you will be given puzzles and challenges to solve as you work your way out of the room. You might need to make decisions about which clues to follow or which objects to use to solve the puzzles.
- Cooking: Plan and cook a meal with your family. You will need to make decisions about what to cook, what ingredients to use, and how to prepare them. For example, you might need to decide between two different recipes or choose which vegetables to use in a stir-fry.
- Lego challenges: Create and complete Lego challenges, which require you to plan, make decisions, and solve problems. You might need to decide which pieces to use to build a certain structure or how to modify a design to make it more stable.
- Create your own game: Design and create your own game, which will require you to make decisions about the rules, challenges, and

objectives. You might need to decide which game mechanics to use or how to balance the difficulty level.

- DIY projects: Take on a DIY project like building a birdhouse or making your own jewelry. You will need to make decisions about what materials to use and how to assemble them. For instance, you might need to decide between using nails or screws or choosing which color beads to use in a bracelet.
- Scavenger hunt: Organize a scavenger hunt where you need to solve clues to find hidden items. You might need to make decisions about which clue to follow next or how to interpret a cryptic message.
- Mystery games: Play mystery games like Clue or Sherlock Holmes Consulting Detective, where you need to solve a mystery by gathering clues and making deductions. You might need to make decisions about which suspects to question or where to look for evidence.
- Science experiments: Conduct science experiments that require you to follow a procedure and make observations. You might need to make decisions about how to record data or which variables to control.
- Outdoor adventures: Plan and go on an outdoor adventure like a hike or camping trip. You will need to make decisions about what equipment to bring, where to set up camp, and what activities to do.
- Art projects: Create art projects like painting or drawing, which require you to make decisions about composition and color. You might need to decide which colors to use in a painting or which elements to include in a drawing.
- Debate: Participate in a debate where you need to make arguments and counterarguments based on evidence and logic. You might need to make decisions about which points to emphasize or how to respond to your opponent's arguments.
- Puzzle-solving games: Play puzzle-solving games like Sudoku or crosswords, which require you to make decisions about which numbers or words to fill in based on logic and deduction. You might need to make decisions about which strategy to use to solve the puzzle.

You've discovered so many new skills to problem-solve and make decisions! From the steps you can take to skills you can practice, you are ready to take on the world and any problem that arrives. In the next chapter, you'll learn how not to get distracted by your worries and fears!

CHAPTER 16
WHAT DOES IT MEAN TO BECOME MORE MINDFUL?

Have you ever been so lost in a fun activity that you forgot about everything else around you? Maybe you were playing with your friends, drawing, or reading a book. You were focused and present in the moment, without any worries about the past or the future. This is what it means to be mindful.

Being mindful means paying attention to the present moment and being fully engaged in what you're doing, without any distractions or judgments. It's a skill that can help you improve your overall well-being, including your mental health, physical health, and relationships with others.

In today's fast-paced world, it's easy to get caught up in stress, anxiety, and worries about the future. As a kid, you might have worries about school, making friends, or fitting in. Being mindful can help you stay calm and focused in the midst of these challenges.

When you practice mindfulness, you can improve your attention, memory, and learning abilities. For example, if you're studying for a test, being mindful can help you stay focused on the material and remember it better. It can also help you become more creative and think outside the box.

Mindfulness can also help you manage your emotions and react more calmly to stressful situations. For example, if you're feeling angry or upset, taking a few deep breaths and being mindful of your thoughts and feelings can help you calm down and make better decisions.

Being mindful can also improve your physical health. When you're stressed, your body produces hormones like cortisol that can harm your immune system, digestion, and sleep. Being mindful can help reduce stress and improve your overall health.

WAYS TO PRACTICE MINDFULNESS

Here are some tips on how to practice mindfulness (Moralis, 2016):

1. Point out what the body feels and describe it: One way to start practicing mindfulness is to focus on your body and the sensations you feel. Take a few deep breaths and notice how your body feels. Are you tense or relaxed? Do you feel any discomfort or pain? By paying attention to how your body feels, you can learn to be more aware of your emotions and find ways to relieve stress or anxiety.

2. Express your emotions in a healthy way: Emotions are a natural part of life, but sometimes they can be overwhelming. Practicing mindfulness means acknowledging and accepting your emotions without judgment. Instead of bottling up your feelings, try expressing them in a healthy way. You can talk to a trusted friend or family member, write in a journal, or even draw or paint your emotions.

3. Take deep breaths: Deep breathing is a simple but effective way to calm your mind and reduce stress. When you feel overwhelmed, take a few slow, deep breaths in through your nose and out through your mouth. You can count to four as you inhale, hold for a second, and then exhale for four counts. Focusing on your breath can help you stay present in the moment and ease anxious thoughts.

4. Move and stretch: Mindfulness doesn't have to be a sedentary activity. You can practice mindfulness while moving and stretching your body. Take a break from sitting at your desk and stretch your arms and legs. Go for a walk or do some yoga poses. Being active can help you release tension and clear your mind.

5. Be aware of your surroundings: Sometimes, we get so caught up in our own thoughts that we forget to pay attention to the world around us. Practicing mindfulness means being fully present in your surroundings. Take a moment to notice the colors and shapes around you, the sounds you hear, and the smells in the air. You might be surprised at what you notice when you take the time to be present.

6. Mindful eating: Eating can be a great opportunity to practice mindfulness. Before you start eating, take a moment to appreciate the food in front of you. Notice the colors and textures, and take a deep breath to smell the aroma. As you eat, pay attention to the taste and texture of each bite.

Chew slowly and savor the flavors. Mindful eating can help you appreciate your food more and be more in tune with your body's hunger and fullness cues.

7. Take a nature walk: Spending time in nature can be a great way to practice mindfulness. Take a walk in a park or go on a hike. As you walk, pay attention to the sights, sounds, and smells around you. Feel the sun on your skin or the wind in your hair. Being in nature can help you feel more connected to the world around you and give you a sense of peace and calm.

Remember, mindfulness is a skill that takes time and practice. Don't worry if you don't get it right away. Just keep trying and you'll find what works best for you. By practicing mindfulness, you can learn to be more present in your life and find peace in even the busiest of moments.

REFLECTING ON WHAT IT MEANS TO BE MINDFUL

1. How do you feel when you practice mindfulness? Describe your emotions and physical sensations.
2. What are some ways you can practice mindfulness during the day, even when you are busy or stressed?
3. What is one thing you are grateful for right now? Why does it bring you joy?
4. Describe a peaceful place you like to go to in your mind when you feel stressed or anxious.
5. How can you use mindfulness to help you cope with difficult emotions like sadness, anger, or frustration?
6. What is one thing you can do today to be kind to yourself and practice self-care?
7. Think about your five senses (sight, sound, smell, taste, touch). Name one thing for each sense that you find soothing or relaxing.
8. What are some things that distract you from being present in the moment? How can you limit those distractions and focus on the present?
9. Describe a time when you felt truly connected to someone or something. What made that moment special?

10. How can you incorporate mindfulness into your daily routine? Brainstorm some ideas for mindfulness activities you can do regularly.

Coming up you will learn all about how you can become more independent and responsible. You will discover tips to show your parents just how trustworthy you are, ways to take on bigger responsibilities, and how to develop yourself as a person!

CHAPTER 17
A GUIDE TO BECOMING MORE RESPONSIBLE AND INDEPENDENT

As a kid, you may often feel like you are not in control of many things in your life. Adults make the rules, decide what you can and cannot do, and generally have more responsibilities than you. However, as you grow older and mature, you may start to feel a desire to take on more responsibility and gain more control over your life. In this chapter, we will explore ways in which you can gain more responsibility as a kid and learn valuable skills that will help you throughout your life. Whether it's taking on household chores, volunteering in your community, or pursuing your passions, there are many ways for you to become more responsible and take charge of your life. So, let's dive in and explore some strategies for gaining more responsibility as a kid!

WAYS YOU CAN GAIN MORE INDEPENDENCE

Chipping in around the house can help you develop more responsibility and independence in many ways. By taking on household chores, you'll be able to contribute to the household and learn valuable life skills that will help you in the future.

For example, doing the dishes may seem like a simple task, but it requires you to be responsible and take initiative. You'll need to figure out how to effectively clean the dishes, and make sure you do a thorough job. By doing this, you'll be developing your problem-solving skills and attention to detail.

Another example is doing laundry. Learning how to properly sort and wash clothes will not only help you contribute to the household but also prepare you for living independently in the future. By doing this, you'll be developing your organizational skills and become better at relying on yourself.

To do these tasks better, you can start by asking your parents or guardians what needs to be done around the house. Take the initiative to offer your help and learn how to do each task properly. You can also create a schedule to help you keep track of what needs to be done and when. This will help you develop a sense of responsibility and ensure that you're regularly contributing.

In addition to these household chores, you can also take on other responsibilities such as volunteering in your community, taking care of a pet, or pursuing your passions. By doing these things, you'll be able to develop your independence, build your confidence, and learn important life skills that will serve you well as you grow older.

By trying new things, developing your passions, and setting and achieving goals, you can become more independent and confident in yourself. Here are some more tips on how to gain independence as a kid (Fraser-Thill, 2022):

Try new things

Trying new things can be scary, but it can also be a great way to gain independence. When you try something new, you're stepping out of your comfort zone and taking control of your own life. It could be trying a new sport, learning a new skill, or making a new friend.

To try new things, start by thinking about something you've always wanted to try. Maybe it's learning to play an instrument, trying new food, or signing up for a new club at school. Once you've decided what you want to try, do some research and figure out how to get started. You can talk to your parents or guardians, search online, or ask a teacher or coach for help.

Develop your passions

Developing your passions is a great way to gain independence because it allows you to pursue something that you're truly interested in. Whether it's playing a sport, writing, painting, or anything else, pursuing your passions will help you feel more confident in yourself and your abilities.

To develop your passions, start by figuring out what you're interested in. Think about the things that make you happy and the activities that you enjoy doing. Once you've identified your passions, set aside time each week to work on them. This could mean practicing your sport, writing in a journal, or taking an art class. By dedicating time to your passions, you'll become more confident and independent in pursuing your interests.

Reach goals and achievements without being asked

Setting and achieving goals is a great way to gain independence and confidence. When you set a goal for yourself and work hard to achieve it, you're taking control of your own life and showing yourself that you're capable of great things.

To set and achieve goals, start by thinking about something you want to accomplish. It could be getting better grades, improving your athletic abilities, or learning a new skill. Once you've identified your goal, break it down into smaller, achievable steps. For example, if your goal is to get better grades, you could set a goal to study for an hour each night and to turn in all of your assignments on time.

Make your own decisions

Making your own decisions is a key part of gaining independence. When you make decisions for yourself, you're taking control of your own life and showing yourself that you're capable of making good choices.

To start making your own decisions, think about something small that you can decide for yourself. It could be choosing what to wear, what to eat for breakfast, or what book to read next. Once you've made a decision, stick with it and see how it feels. As you become more comfortable with making decisions, you can start making bigger decisions, such as choosing which after-school activities to participate in or what classes to take.

Learn new skills

Learning new skills is a great way to gain independence and confidence. When you learn a new skill, you're showing yourself that you're capable of growth and development.

To learn new skills, start by thinking about something you're interested in learning. It could be a new language, a new musical instrument, or a new type of art. Once you've identified what you want to learn, find resources to help you get started. You can search online, ask a teacher or coach, or sign up for a class.

Take responsibility for your actions

Taking responsibility for your actions is an important part of gaining independence. When you take responsibility for your actions, you're showing yourself that you're in control of your own life and that you're capable of making good choices.

To take responsibility for your actions, start by acknowledging when you've made a mistake. Instead of blaming someone else or making excuses, take ownership of your actions and apologize if necessary. You can also take steps to make things right, such as fixing something you've broken or making up for something you've done wrong.

Manage your time

Managing your time is a crucial part of gaining independence. When you're able to manage your time effectively, you can prioritize the things that are important to you and make the most of your day.

To manage your time, start by making a schedule or a to-do list. Write down the things you need to do each day and prioritize them based on importance. You can also use a calendar or planner to keep track of important dates and deadlines. By managing your time effectively, you'll be able to accomplish more and feel more in control of your own life.

Communicate effectively

Effective communication is an important part of gaining independence. When you're able to communicate effectively, you can express your thoughts and feelings clearly and confidently.

To communicate effectively, start by listening actively when someone else is speaking. Show that you're paying attention by making eye contact and asking questions if you don't understand something. When it's your turn to speak, express your thoughts and feelings clearly and respectfully. Use "I" statements instead of "you" statements, and avoid blaming or attacking others.

In conclusion, gaining independence as a kid is all about taking control of your own life and showing yourself that you're capable of great things. By trying new things, developing your passions, setting and achieving goals, making your own decisions, learning new skills, taking responsibility for your actions, managing your time, and communicating effectively, you'll become more confident and independent in all areas of your life. Remember, independence is a journey, not a destination. Keep pushing yourself and trying new things, and you'll be amazed at what you can accomplish!

FINAL WORDS

Congratulations! You have reached the end of this book on life skills, and you should feel incredibly proud of yourself. By learning and practicing these skills, you have gained powerful tools that will help you navigate the world and become more independent.

Throughout this book, you have learned how to make friends, develop your social skills, handle big emotions, recognize and resist peer pressure, show empathy for others, and succeed in school. You have learned how to communicate effectively, manage your time, set and achieve goals, take responsibility for your actions, and so much more.

All of these skills are incredibly important, and they will serve you well throughout your life. Whether you're starting a new school, making new friends, or facing a tough challenge, you can draw on these skills to help you succeed.

But remember, learning these skills is just the beginning. To truly become independent, you need to practice these skills every day. The more you practice, the better you'll get, and the more confident and independent you'll become.

So keep practicing, keep pushing yourself, and don't be afraid to try new things. With these skills in your toolkit, you are ready to take on the world and accomplish great things. Remember, you are powerful, you are capable, and you are ready to succeed!

Thanks for reading. If you enjoyed this book, please consider leaving an honest review.

ALSO BY GRACE DANIELS

Life Skills for Teenage Girls

Life Skills for Teenage Boys

The Growth Mindset for Kids

The Growth Mindset for Teens

<u>Coming Soon:</u>

Building Confident, Brave and Beautiful Girls

Inspring Stories for Confident, Brave and Beautiful Girls

Inspring Stories for Kind, Confident and Brave Boys

Career Planning for Teens

Social Skills for Teens

REFERENCES

Eisenberg, B. (2016, February 10). *12 skills and 5 household chores that can serve as preparation for future vocation.* Friendship Circle / Resources. Retrieved March 28, 2023, from https://www.friendshipcircle.org/blog/2016/02/10/12-skills-and-5-household-chores-that-can-serve-as-preparation-for-future-vocation

Fraser-Thill, R. (2022, January 18). *How parents can teach their tween responsibilities for life.* Verywell Family. Retrieved March 28, 2023, from https://www.verywellfamily.com/teaching-responsibility-to-your-child-3288496

Garey, J. (2022, August 18). *Teaching kids how to deal with conflict.* Child Mind Institute. Retrieved March 25, 2023, from https://childmind.org/article/teaching-kids-how-to-deal-with-conflict/

GreatSchools, 2022 P. article. (2022, December 17). *6 ways to help your child deal with Peer Pressure.* Parenting. Retrieved March 25, 2023, from https://www.greatschools.org/gk/articles/6-tips-resisting-peer-pressure/

Heart and Stroke. (2023). *10 kitchen skills every 10-year-old should know.* Heart and Stroke Foundation of Canada. Retrieved March 28, 2023, from https://www.heartandstroke.ca/articles/10-kitchen-skills-every-10-year-old-should-know

Homer. (2021). *Social Skills for Kids.* HOMER Blog I The essential early learning program for ages 28 Try it free. Retrieved March 25, 2023, from https://www.learnwithhomer.com/homer-blog/4190/social-skills-for-kids/

Jacobs, R. (2014, August 16). *Teaching my child first aid: 6 essentials.* Eartheasy Guides & Articles. Retrieved March 28, 2023, from https://learn.eartheasy.com/articles/teaching-my-child-first-aid-6-essentials/

Mattingly, J. (2020, November 30). *Developing problem-solving skills for kids: Strategies & tips.* Kodable. Retrieved March 28, 2023, from https://www.kodable.com/learn/problem-solving-skills-for-kids

Moralis, S. (2016, May 2). *12 simple ways to teach mindfulness to kids.* Psychology Today. Retrieved March 28, 2023, from https://www.psychologytoday.com/us/blog/breathe-mama-breathe/201605/12-simple-ways-teach-mindfulness-kids

Morin, A. (2021, April 25). *How to help a highly emotional child cope with big feelings.* Verywell Family. Retrieved March 25, 2023, from https://www.verywellfamily.com/how-to-help-an-overly-emotional-child-4157594#:~:text=Validate%20and%20Relate&text=It's%20not%20a%20big%20deal,they%20feel%20and%20be%20empathetic.

Northwestern Medicine. (n.d.). *Personal Hygiene for Kids.* Northwestern Medicine. Retrieved March 27, 2023, from https://www.nm.org/healthbeat/healthy-tips/emotional-health/Personal-Hygiene-for-Kids

Williamson, N. (2021, June 29). *How to explain and teach empathy to a child.* As They Grow. Retrieved March 25, 2023, from https://www.as-they-grow.com/how-to-explain-and-teach-empathy-to-a-child#h-how-to-explain-empathy-to-a-child

REFERENCES

Image Credit: Shutterstock.com

Made in United States
Troutdale, OR
06/12/2023

10575427R00084